VITAL
IDEAS
WORK

Other books in the VITAL IDEAS series:

VITAL IDEAS: Crime
Edited by Theresa Starkey

VITAL IDEAS: Money
Edited by Dana Heller and Claire Pamplin

VITAL IDEAS: Sex
Edited by Regina Barreca

Series Editor: Daniel Born, academic department chair in Kaplan University's legal studies department and lecturer in the MA literature program at Northwestern University's School of Continuing Studies

Volume Editor: Christina Boufis, director of the Writing Program at the San Francisco Art Institute.

Contributors
Kristine Bergman
Nancy Carr
Steven Craig
Patrick Hurley
Mary Klein
Dylan Nelson
Amy Schuler
Donald H. Whitfield
Mary Williams

Edited by Christina Boufis

THE GREAT BOOKS FOUNDATION
A nonprofit educational organization

Published and distributed by

THE GREAT BOOKS FOUNDATION
A nonprofit educational organization

35 E. Wacker Drive, Suite 400
Chicago, Illinois 60601
www.greatbooks.org

Shared Inquiry™ is a trademark of the Great Books Foundation.
The contents of this publication include proprietary trademarks
and copyrighted materials and may be used or quoted only with
permission and appropriate credit to the Foundation.

First printing
9 8 7 6 5 4 3 2 1

Library of Congress Cataloging-in-Publication Data

Vital ideas : work / edited by Christina Boufis.
     p. cm.
 ISBN 978-1-933147-78-9 (alk. paper)
 1. Work. 2. Inquiry-based learning. I. Boufis, Christina. II.
Title: Work.
 HD4904.V58 2011
 331--dc23
                                    2011028116

Book cover and interior design: THINK Book Works

About the
Great Books Foundation

The Great Books Foundation, publisher of the Vital Ideas series, was established in 1947 by University of Chicago educators Robert Maynard Hutchins and Mortimer Adler. The Foundation is an independent, nonprofit educational organization whose mission is to empower readers of all ages to become more reflective and responsible thinkers. To this end, the Foundation publishes enduring works across the disciplines and conducts workshops in Shared Inquiry,™ a text-based, Socratic method of learning.

Contents

Preface

Work. We sometimes think of it as so important that it is almost a religious calling; at other times it strikes us as a necessary evil in a world of toil and struggle, a force that saps our energy and drains our souls. In this volume of the Vital Ideas series, we encounter a variety of voices that explore the concept of work in timeless and yet fresh ways: a veteran journalist who goes to work as a restaurant server and writes about the experience; a young man who works the Christmas season as one of Santa's elves in a department store; a fabulously successful Internet entrepreneur who helped invent Hotmail. Through fiction, poetry, memoir, and philosophical essay, the authors of these selections explore and wrestle with the meaning of an activity that dominates so much of our waking lives.

The Vital Ideas series takes a content-based rather than skills-based approach to reading and composition. It is based on the conviction, supported by the editors' own classroom experience, that students are most motivated to improve their reading and writing skills when they are engaged with subject matter that is meaningful to them. The contents of each volume represent outstanding examples of well-reasoned thought and high-quality writing across a variety of genres. In keeping with the tradition of the Great Books Foundation, the Vital Ideas series is first and foremost designed to stimulate rewarding Shared Inquiry discussions and instill the habits of reflective, critical thinking.

Using the Questions

Each of the selections in this volume is followed by two sets of questions that will help enrich the reader's engagement with what the author has to say.

The "For Discussion" questions ask about the meaning of what the author says, often referring to a specific phrase or passage in the selection. These questions ask readers to form interpretations of the text and are particularly helpful for initiating classroom discussion. They are closely connected with the practice of Shared Inquiry discussion, described at the back of this volume in the "About Shared Inquiry" section.

The questions designated "For Further Reflection" generally ask for a broader response to the selection. These questions work well in conjunction with the "For Discussion" questions but can also be used as prompts for writing assignments, since they encourage not only interpretations of the text, but also the evaluation of its ideas.

In addition, at the back of the book is a set of "Comparison Questions." These questions encourage discussion and writing about issues that are common to two or more selections in the book. Unlike the generic "compare and contrast" questions in many textbooks, the "Comparison Questions" ask readers to critically address specific ideas and points of view that the authors have expressed.

Tillie Olsen (1912?–2007) was born in Omaha, Nebraska, the daughter of politically active Jewish immigrants. Olsen dropped out of high school to work, joined the Young Communist League at eighteen, held a number of low-paying jobs, and was twice arrested for her political work. Believing that art should serve political and social ends, Olsen wrote short stories and poems reflecting the turbulent world of America in the 1930s. But she wrote little between the mid-1930s and the early 1950s, devoting herself to raising her four daughters and working to support her family and her political causes. After she resumed writing, she received a Stanford University fellowship, which enabled her to write and publish the four stories collected in *Tell Me a Riddle* (1961). She is also the author of a novel, *Yonnondio* (1974), and *Silences* (1978), a collection of essays about the social, economic, and familial obstacles that writers face.

I Stand Here Ironing

I stand here ironing, and what you asked me moves tormented back and forth with the iron.

"I wish you would manage the time to come in and talk with me about your daughter. I'm sure you can help me understand her. She's a youngster who needs help and whom I'm deeply interested in helping."

"Who needs help." . . . Even if I came, what good would it do? You think because I am her mother I have a key, or that in some way you could use me as a key? She has lived for nineteen years. There is all that life that has happened outside of me, beyond me.

And when is there time to remember, to sift, to weigh, to estimate, to total? I will start and there will be an interruption and I will have to gather it all together again. Or I will become engulfed with all I did or did not do, with what should have been and what cannot be helped.

She was a beautiful baby. The first and only one of our five that was beautiful at birth. You do not guess how new and uneasy her tenancy in her now-loveliness. You did not know her all those years she was thought homely, or see her poring over her baby pictures, making me tell her over and over how beautiful she had been—and would be, I would tell her—and was now, to the seeing eye. But the seeing eyes were few or non-existent. Including mine.

I nursed her. They feel that's important nowadays. I nursed all the children, but with her, with all the fierce rigidity of first motherhood, I did like the books then said. Though her cries battered me to trembling and my breasts ached with swollenness, I waited till the clock decreed.

Why do I put that first? I do not even know if it matters, or if it explains anything.

She was a beautiful baby. She blew shining bubbles of sound. She loved motion, loved light, loved color and music and textures. She would lie on the floor in her blue overalls patting the surface so hard in ecstasy her hands and feet would blur. She was a miracle to me, but when she was eight months old I had to leave her daytimes with the woman downstairs to whom she was no miracle at all, for I worked or looked for work and for Emily's father, who "could no longer endure" (he wrote in his goodbye note) "sharing want with us."

I was nineteen. It was the prerelief, pre-WPA world of the depression. I would start running as soon as I got off the streetcar, running up the stairs, the place smelling sour, and awake or asleep to startle awake, when she saw me she would break into a clogged weeping that could not be comforted, a weeping I can hear yet.

After a while I found a job hashing at night so I could be with her days, and it was better. But it came to where I had to bring her to his family and leave her.

It took a long time to raise the money for her fare back. Then she got chicken pox and I had to wait longer. When she finally came, I hardly knew her, walking quick and nervous like her father, looking like her father, thin, and dressed in a shoddy red that yellowed her skin and glared at the pockmarks. All the baby loveliness gone.

She was two. Old enough for nursery school they said, and I did not know then what I know now—the fatigue of the long day, and the lacerations of group life in the kinds of nurseries that are only parking places for children.

Except that it would have made no difference if I had known. It was the only place there was. It was the only way we could be together, the only way I could hold a job.

And even without knowing, I knew. I knew the teacher that was evil because all these years it has curdled into my memory, the little boy hunched in the corner, her rasp, "Why aren't you outside, because Alvin hits you? That's no reason, go out, scaredy." I knew Emily hated it even if she did not clutch and implore "don't go Mommy" like the other children, mornings.

She always had a reason why we should stay home. Momma, you look sick. Momma, I feel sick. Momma, the teachers aren't there today, they're sick. Momma, we can't go, there was a fire there last night. Momma, it's a holiday today, no school, they told me.

But never a direct protest, never rebellion. I think of our others in their three-, four-year-oldness—the explosions, the tempers, the denunciations, the demands—and I feel suddenly ill. I put the iron down. What in me demanded that goodness in her? And what was the cost, the cost to her of such goodness?

The old man living in the back once said in his gentle way: "You should smile at Emily more when you look at her." What *was* in my face when I looked at her? I loved her. There were all the acts of love.

It was only with the others I remembered what he said, and it was the face of joy, and not of care or tightness or worry I turned to them—too late for Emily. She does not smile easily, let alone almost always as her brothers and sisters do. Her face is closed and somber, but when she wants, how fluid. You must have seen it in her pantomimes, you spoke of her rare gift for comedy on the stage that rouses a laughter out of the audience so dear they applaud and applaud and do not want to let her go.

Where does it come from, that comedy? There was none of it in her when she came back to me that second time, after I had had to send her away again. She had a new daddy now to learn to love, and I think perhaps it was a better time.

Except when we left her alone nights, telling ourselves she was old enough.

"Can't you go some other time, Mommy, like tomorrow?" she would ask. "Will it be just a little while you'll be gone? Do you promise?"

The time we came back, the front door open, the clock on the floor in the hall. She rigid awake. "It wasn't just a little while. I didn't cry. Three times I called you, just three times, and then I ran downstairs to open the door so you could come faster. The clock talked loud. I threw it away, it scared me what it talked."

She said the clock talked loud again that night I went to the hospital to have Susan. She was delirious with the fever that comes before red measles, but she was fully conscious all the week I was gone and the week after we were home when she could not come near the new baby or me.

She did not get well. She stayed skeleton thin, not wanting to eat, and night after night she had nightmares. She would call for me, and I would rouse from exhaustion to sleepily call back: "You're all right, darling, go to sleep, it's just a dream," and if she still called, in a sterner voice, "Now go to sleep, Emily, there's nothing to hurt you." Twice, only twice, when I had to get up for Susan anyhow, I went in to sit with her.

Now when it is too late (as if she would let me hold and comfort her like I do the others) I get up and go to her at once at her moan or restless stirring. "Are you awake, Emily? Can I get you something?" And the answer is always the same: "No, I'm all right, go back to sleep, Mother."

They persuaded me at the clinic to send her away to a convalescent home in the country where "she can have the kind of food and care you can't manage for her, and you'll be free to concentrate on the new baby." They still send children to that place. I see pictures on the society page of sleek young women planning affairs to raise money for it, or dancing at the affairs, or decorating Easter eggs or filling Christmas stockings for the children.

They never have a picture of the children so I do not know if the girls still wear those gigantic red bows and the ravaged looks on the every other Sunday when parents can come to visit "unless otherwise notified"—as we were notified the first six weeks.

Oh it is a handsome place, green lawns and tall trees and fluted flower beds. High up on the balconies of each cottage the children stand, the girls in their red bows and white dresses, the boys in white suits and giant red ties. The parents stand below shrieking up to be heard and the children shriek down to be heard, and between them the invisible wall "Not To Be Contaminated by Parental Germs or Physical Affection."

There was a tiny girl who always stood hand in hand with Emily. Her parents never came. One visit she was gone. "They moved her to Rose Cottage" Emily shouted in explanation. "They don't like you to love anybody here."

She wrote once a week, the labored writing of a seven-year-old. "I am fine. How is the baby. If I write my leter nicly I will have a star. Love." There never was a star. We wrote every other day, letters she could never hold or keep but only hear read—once. "We simply do not have room for children to keep any personal possessions," they patiently explained when we pieced one Sunday's shrieking together to plead how much it would mean to Emily, who loved to keep things, to be allowed to keep her letters and cards.

Each visit she looked frailer. "She isn't eating," they told us.

(They had runny eggs for breakfast or mush with lumps, Emily said later, I'd hold it in my mouth and not swallow. Nothing ever tasted good, just when they had chicken.)

It took us eight months to get her released home, and only the fact that she gained back so little of her seven lost pounds convinced the social worker.

I used to try to hold and love her after she came back, but her body would stay stiff, and after a while she'd push away. She ate little. Food sickened her, and I think much of life too. Oh she had physical lightness and brightness, twinkling by on skates, bouncing like a ball up and down up and down over the jump rope, skimming over the hill; but these were momentary.

She fretted about her appearance, thin and dark and foreign-looking at a time when every little girl was supposed to look or thought she should look a chubby blonde replica of Shirley Temple. The doorbell sometimes rang for her, but no one seemed to come and play in the house or be a best friend. Maybe because we moved so much.

There was a boy she loved painfully through two school semesters. Months later she told me how she had taken pennies from my purse to buy him candy. "Licorice was his favorite and I brought him some every day, but he still liked Jennifer better'n me. Why,

Mommy?" The kind of question for which there was no answer.

School was a worry to her. She was not glib or quick in a world where glibness and quickness were easily confused with ability to learn. To her overworked and exasperated teachers she was an overconscientious "slow learner" who kept trying to catch up and was absent entirely too often.

I let her be absent, though sometimes the illness was imaginary. How different from my now-strictness about attendance with the others. I wasn't working. We had a new baby, I was home anyhow. Sometimes, after Susan grew old enough, I would keep her home from school, too, to have them all together.

Mostly Emily had asthma, and her breathing, harsh and labored, would fill the house with a curiously tranquil sound. I would bring the two old dresser mirrors and her boxes of collections to her bed. She would select beads and single earrings, bottle tops and shells, dried flowers and pebbles, old postcards and scraps, all sorts of oddments; then she and Susan would play Kingdom, setting up landscapes and furniture, peopling them with action.

Those were the only times of peaceful companionship between her and Susan. I have edged away from it, that poisonous feeling between them, that terrible balancing of hurts and needs I had to do between the two, and did so badly, those earlier years.

Oh there are conflicts between the others too, each one human, needing, demanding, hurting, taking—but only between Emily and Susan, no, Emily toward Susan that corroding resentment. It seems so obvious on the surface, yet it is not obvious. Susan, the second child, Susan, golden- and curly-haired and chubby, quick and articulate and assured, everything in appearance and manner Emily was not; Susan, not able to resist Emily's precious things, losing or sometimes clumsily breaking them; Susan telling jokes and riddles to company for applause while Emily sat silent (to say to me later: that was *my* riddle, Mother, I told it to Susan); Susan, who for all of five years' difference in age was just a year behind Emily in developing physically.

I am glad for that slow physical development that widened the difference between her and her contemporaries, though she suffered over it. She was too vulnerable for that terrible world of youthful competition, of preening and parading, of constant measuring of yourself against every other, of envy, "If I had that copper hair," "If I had that skin. . . ." She tormented herself enough about not looking like the others, there was enough of the unsureness, the having to be conscious of words before you speak, the constant caring—what are they thinking of me? without having it all magnified by the merciless physical drives.

Ronnie is calling. He is wet and I changed him. It is rare there is such a cry now. That time of motherhood is almost behind me when the ear is not one's own but must always be racked and listening for the child cry, the child call. We sit for a while and I hold him, looking out over the city spread in charcoal with its soft aisles of light. "*Shoogily,*" he breathes and curls closer. I carry him back to bed, asleep. *Shoogily.* A funny word, a family word, inherited from Emily, invented by her to say: *comfort.*

In this and other ways she leaves her seal, I say aloud. And startle at my saying it. What do I mean? What did I start to gather together, to try and make coherent? I was at the terrible, growing years. War years. I do not remember them well. I was working, there were four smaller ones now, there was not time for her. She had to help be a mother, and housekeeper, and shopper. She had to set her seal. Mornings of crisis and near hysteria trying to get lunches packed, hair combed, coats and shoes found, everyone to school or child care on time, the baby ready for transportation. And always the paper scribbled on by a smaller one, the book looked at by Susan then mislaid, the homework not done. Running out to that huge school where she was one, she was lost, she was a drop; suffering over her unpreparedness, stammering and unsure in her classes.

There was so little time left at night after the kids were bedded down. She would struggle over books, always eating (it was in those years she developed her enormous appetite that is legendary in our family) and I would be ironing, or preparing food for the next day, or writing V-mail to Bill, or tending the baby. Sometimes, to make me laugh, or out of her despair, she would imitate happenings or types at school.

I think I said once: "Why don't you do something like this in the school amateur show?" One morning she phoned me at work, hardly understandable through the weeping: "Mother, I did it. I won, I won; they gave me first prize; they clapped and clapped and wouldn't let me go."

Now suddenly she was Somebody, and as imprisoned in her difference as she had been in her anonymity.

She began to be asked to perform at other high schools, even in colleges, then at city and statewide affairs. The first one we went to, I only recognized her that first moment when thin, shy, she almost drowned herself into the curtains. Then: Was this Emily? The control, the command, the convulsing and deadly clowning, the spell, then the roaring, stamping audience, unwilling to let this rare and precious laughter out of their lives.

Afterwards: You ought to do something about her with a gift like that—but without money or knowing how, what does one do? We have left it all to her, and the gift has as often eddied inside, clogged and clotted, as been used and growing.

She is coming. She runs up the stairs two at a time with her light graceful step, and I know she is happy tonight. Whatever it was that occasioned your call did not happen today.

"Aren't you ever going to finish the ironing, Mother? Whistler painted his mother a rocker. I'd have to paint mine to standing over an ironing board." This is one of her communicative nights and she tells me everything and nothing as she fixes herself a plate of food out of the icebox.

She is so lovely. Why did you want me to come in at all? Why were you concerned? She will find her way.

She starts up the stairs to bed. "Don't get *me* up with the rest in the morning." "But I thought you were having midterms." "Oh, those," she comes back in, kisses me, and says quite lightly, "in a couple of years when we'll all be atom-dead they won't matter a bit."

She has said it before. She *believes* it. But because I have been dredging the past, and all that compounds a human being is so heavy and meaningful to me, I cannot endure it tonight.

I will never total it all. I will never come in to say: She was a child seldom smiled at. Her father left me before she was a year old. I had to work her first six years when there was work, or I sent her home and to his relatives. There were years she had care she hated. She was dark and thin and foreign-looking in a world where the prestige went to blondness and curly hair and dimples, she was slow where glibness was prized. She was a child of anxious, not proud, love. We were poor and could not afford for her the soil of easy growth. I was a young mother, I was a distracted mother. There were the other children pushing up, demanding. Her younger sister seemed all that she was not There were years she did not let me touch her. She kept too much in herself, her life was such she had to keep too much in herself. My wisdom came too late. She has much to her and probably little will come of it. She is a child of her age, of depression, of war, of fear.

Let her be. So all that is in her will not bloom—but in how many does it? There is still enough left to live by. Only help her to know—help make it so there is cause for her to know—that she is more than this dress on the ironing board, helpless before the iron.

FOR DISCUSSION

1. Why does the narrator compose her response to the call about her daughter while she is ironing? Why does she think the question in the note moves "tormented back and forth with the iron"? (5)

2. Why does the narrator feel sick when she thinks about how Emily never rebelled or protested as a child? Why does the narrator wonder "what was the cost, the cost to her of such goodness"? (7)

3. What does the narrator mean when she says that Emily "leaves her seal"? (12) How does she feel about how much Emily had to participate in raising her younger siblings?

4. How much does the narrator blame herself for the difficulties she had raising Emily, and how much does she blame economic circumstances beyond her control?

FOR FURTHER REFLECTION

1. Do you agree with the narrator that Emily will be all right even though "all that is in her will not bloom"? (15)

2. What does "I Stand Here Ironing" suggest about poverty's causes and effects? Do you agree?

Philip Levine (1928–) was born in Detroit to working-class Russian Jewish immigrants. He graduated from Wayne State University in 1950 and worked at various industrial jobs before earning an MFA from the University of Iowa and beginning to teach at the college level. His first collection of poems, *On the Edge* (1963), celebrates the working-class people of his youth. Levine has said he writes poetry "for people for whom there is no poetry." Levine is known for his urban and often gritty settings and his somber and unpretentious style. He has written many other books of poetry, including *They Feed They Lion* (1972); *What Work Is* (1991), which won the National Book Award; and *The Simple Truth* (1994), which won the Pulitzer Prize. Levine is also the author of *The Bread of Time: Toward an Autobiography* (1994).

What Work Is

We stand in the rain in a long line
waiting at Ford Highland Park. For work.
You know what work is—if you're
old enough to read this you know what
work is, although you may not do it.
Forget you. This is about waiting,
shifting from one foot to another.
Feeling the light rain falling like mist
into your hair, blurring your vision
until you think you see your own brother
ahead of you, maybe ten places.
You rub your glasses with your fingers,
and of course it's someone else's brother,
narrower across the shoulders than
yours but with the same sad slouch, the grin
that does not hide the stubbornness,
the sad refusal to give in to
rain, to the hours wasted waiting,
to the knowledge that somewhere ahead
a man is waiting who will say, "No,
we're not hiring today," for any
reason he wants. You love your brother,
now suddenly you can hardly stand
the love flooding you for your brother,
who's not beside you or behind or
ahead because he's home trying to
sleep off a miserable night shift
at Cadillac so he can get up

before noon to study his German.
Works eight hours a night so he can sing
Wagner, the opera you hate most,
the worst music ever invented.
How long has it been since you told him
you loved him, held his wide shoulders,
opened your eyes wide and said those words,
and maybe kissed his cheek? You've never
done something so simple, so obvious,
not because you're too young or too dumb,
not because you're jealous or even mean
or incapable of crying in
the presence of another man, no,
just because you don't know what work is.

FOR DISCUSSION

1. At the beginning of the poem, why does the speaker say, "You know what work is" and then, "Forget you"? (19)

2. Why are we told that the man in the line "can hardly stand" the love flooding him for his brother? (19)

3. Why has the man in the line never "done something so simple, so obvious" as telling his brother he loves him? (20)

4. Why does the speaker conclude that the man in the line has never told his brother he loves him just because the man doesn't know what work is?

FOR FURTHER REFLECTION

1. What does it mean to "know what work is"? (19) How is this knowledge connected to loving or appreciating people?

2. What qualities does this poem celebrate in people who stand in line to wait for work? How does Levine want us to feel about the people waiting in line?

Barbara Ehrenreich (1941–) was born in Butte, Montana.
Though both her BA and PhD are in the sciences, she became
a social critic and jounalist, writing essays, articles, and books
about subjects that fascinate her. She is a passionate activist in
the areas of health care, peace, women's rights, and economic
justice. She is best known for *Nickel and Dimed: On (Not) Getting By
in America* (2001) and is the author of many other books, including
Fear of Falling: The Inner Life of the Middle Class (1989), which was
nominated for a National Book Critics' Circle Award in 1989, and
Bright-Sided (2009), which explores the positive-thinking movement
in America. This selection is taken from an article that appeared
in *Harper's Magazine* and was later adapted to become the first
chapter of *Nickel and Dimed*.

Nickel and Dimed
(selection)

At the beginning of June 1998 I leave behind everything that normally soothes the ego and sustains the body—home, career, companion, reputation, ATM card—for a plunge into the low-wage workforce. There, I became another, occupationally much diminished "Barbara Ehrenreich"—depicted on job-application forms as a divorced homemaker whose sole work experience consists of housekeeping in a few private homes. I am terrified, at the beginning, of being unmasked for what I am: a middle-class journalist setting out to explore the world that welfare mothers are entering, at the rate of approximately 50,000 a month, as welfare reform kicks in. Happily, though, my fears turn out to be entirely unwarranted: during a month of poverty and toil, my name goes unnoticed and for the most part unuttered. In this parallel universe where my father never got out of the mines and I never got through college, I am "baby," "honey," "blondie," and, most commonly, "girl."

My first task is to find a place to live. I figure that if I can earn $7 an hour—which, from the want ads, seems doable—I can afford to spend $500 on rent, or maybe, with severe economies, $600. In the Key West area, where I live, this pretty much confines me to flophouses and trailer homes—like the one, a pleasing fifteen-minute drive from town, that has no air conditioning, no screens, no fans, no television, and, by way of diversion, only the challenge of evading the landlord's Doberman pinscher. The big problem with this

place, though, is the rent, which at $675 a month is well
beyond my reach. All right, Key West is expensive. But
so is New York City, or the Bay Area, or Jackson Hole,
or Telluride, or Boston, or any other place where tourists
and the wealthy compete for living space with the people
who clean their toilets and fry their hash browns.[1] Still,
it is a shock to realize that "trailer trash" has become, for
me, a demographic category to aspire to.

So I decide to make the common trade-off between
affordability and convenience, and go for a $500-a-
month efficiency thirty miles up a two-lane highway
from the employment opportunities of Key West,
meaning forty-five minutes if there's no road construction and I don't get caught behind some sun-dazed
Canadian tourists. I hate the drive, along a roadside
studded with white crosses commemorating the
more effective head-on collisions, but it's a sweet little
place—a cabin, more or less, set in the swampy back yard
of the converted mobile home where my landlord, an
affable TV repairman, lives with his bartender girlfriend.
Anthropologically speaking, a bustling trailer park
would be preferable, but here I have a gleaming white
floor and a firm mattress, and the few resident bugs are
easily vanquished.

Besides, I am not doing this for the anthropology. My
aim is nothing so mistily subjective as to "experience

---

1. According to the Department of Housing and Urban Development, the "fair-market rent" for an efficiency is $551 here in
Monroe County, Florida. A comparable rent in the five
boroughs of New York City is $704; in San Francisco, $713;
and in the heart of Silicon Valley, $808. The fair-market rent
for an area is defined as the amount that would be needed to
pay rent plus utilities for "privately owned, decent, safe, and
sanitary rental housing of a modest (non-luxury) nature with
suitable amenities."

poverty" or find out how it "really feels" to be a long-term low-wage worker. I've had enough unchosen encounters with poverty and the world of low-wage work to know it's not a place you want to visit for touristic purposes; it just smells too much like fear. And with all my real-life assets—bank account, IRA, health insurance, multiroom home—waiting indulgently in the background, I am, of course, thoroughly insulated from the terrors that afflict the genuinely poor.

No, this is a purely objective, scientific sort of mission. The humanitarian rationale for welfare reform—as opposed to the more punitive and stingy impulses that may actually have motivated it—is that work will lift poor women out of poverty while simultaneously inflating their self-esteem and hence their future value in the labor market. Thus, whatever the hassles involved in finding childcare, transportation, etc., the transition from welfare to work will end happily, in greater prosperity for all. Now there are many problems with this comforting prediction, such as the fact that the economy will inevitably undergo a downturn, eliminating many jobs. Even without a downturn, the influx of a million former welfare recipients into the low-wage labor market could depress wages by as much as 11.9 percent, according to the Economic Policy Institute (EPI) in Washington, D.C.

But is it really possible to make a living on the kinds of jobs currently available to unskilled people? Mathematically, the answer is no, as can be shown by taking $6 to $7 an hour, perhaps subtracting a dollar or two an hour for child-care, multiplying by 160 hours a month, and comparing the result to the prevailing rents. According to the National Coalition for the Homeless, for example, in 1998 it took, on average nationwide, an hourly wage of $8.89 to afford a one-bedroom apartment, and the Preamble Center for Public Policy estimates that the odds against a typical welfare recipient's landing a job at such a "living wage" are about 97 to 1. If these numbers are right, low-wage work is not a solution to poverty and possibly not even to homelessness.

It may seem excessive to put this proposition to an experimental test. As certain family members keep unhelpfully reminding me, the viability of low-wage work could be tested, after a fashion, without ever leaving my study. I could just pay myself $7 an hour for eight hours a day, charge myself for room and board, and total up the numbers after a month. Why leave the people and work that I love? But I am an experimental scientist by training. In that business, you don't just sit at a desk and theorize; you plunge into the everyday chaos of nature, where surprises lurk in the most mundane measurements. Maybe, when I got into it, I would discover some hidden economies in the world of the low-wage worker. After all, if 30 percent of the workforce toils for less than $8 an hour, according to the EPI, they may have found some tricks as yet unknown to me. Maybe—who knows?—I would even be able to detect in myself the bracing psychological effects of getting out of the house, as promised by the welfare wonks at places like the Heritage Foundation. Or, on the other hand, maybe there would be unexpected costs—physical, mental, or financial—to throw off all my calculations. Ideally, I should do this with two small children in tow, that being the welfare average, but mine are grown and no one is willing to lend me theirs for a month-long vacation in penury. So this is not the perfect experiment, just a test of the best possible case: an unencumbered woman, smart and even strong, attempting to live more or less off the land.

On the morning of my first full day of job searching, I take a red pen to the want ads, which are auspiciously numerous. Everyone in Key West's booming "hospitality industry" seems to be looking for someone like me—trainable, flexible, and with suitably humble expectations as to pay. I know I possess certain traits that might be advantageous—I'm white and, I like to think, well-spoken and poised—but I decide on two rules: One, I cannot use any skills derived from my education or usual work—not that there are a lot of want ads for satirical essayists anyway. Two, I have to take the best-paid job that is offered me and of course do my best to hold it; no Marxist rants or sneaking off to read novels in the ladies' room. In addition, I rule out various occupations for one reason or another: Hotel front-desk clerk, for example, which to my surprise is regarded as unskilled and pays around $7 an hour, gets eliminated because it involves standing in one spot for eight hours a day. Waitressing is similarly something I'd like to avoid, because I remember it leaving me bone tired when I was eighteen, and I'm decades of varicosities and back pain beyond that now. Telemarketing, one of the first refuges of the suddenly indigent, can be dismissed on grounds of personality. This leaves certain supermarket jobs, such as deli clerk, or housekeeping in Key West's thousands of hotel and guest rooms. Housekeeping is especially appealing, for reasons both atavistic and practical: it's what my mother did before I came along, and it can't be too different from what I've been doing part-time, in my own home, all my life.

So I put on what I take to be a respectful looking outfit of ironed Bermuda shorts and scooped-neck T-shirt and set out for a tour of the local hotels and supermarkets. Best Western, Econo Lodge, and HoJo's all let me fill out application forms, and these are, to my relief, interested in little more than whether I am a legal resident of the United States and have committed any felonies. My next stop is Winn-Dixie, the supermarket, which turns out to have a particularly onerous application process, featuring a fifteen-minute "interview" by computer since, apparently, no human on the premises is deemed capable of representing the corporate point of view. I am conducted to a large room decorated with posters illustrating how to look "professional" (it helps to be white and, if female, permed) and warning of the slick promises that union organizers might try to tempt me with. The interview is multiple choice: Do I have anything, such as childcare problems, that might make it hard for me to get to work on time? Do I think safety on the job is the responsibility of management? Then, popping up cunningly out of the blue: How many dollars' worth of stolen goods have I purchased in the last year? Would I turn in a fellow employee if I caught him stealing? Finally, "Are you an honest person?"

Apparently, I ace the interview, because I am told that all I have to do is show up in some doctor's office tomorrow for a urine test. This seems to be a fairly general rule: if you want to stack Cheerio boxes or vacuum hotel rooms in chemically fascist America, you have to be willing to squat down and pee in front of some health worker (who has no doubt had to do the same thing herself). The wages Winn-Dixie is offering—$6 and a couple of dimes to start with—are not enough, I decide, to compensate for this indignity.[2]

---

2. According to the *Monthly Labor Review* (November 1996), 28 percent of work sites surveyed in the service industry conduct drug tests (corporate workplaces have much higher rates), and the incidence of testing has risen markedly since the eighties. The rate of testing is highest in the South (56 percent of work sites polled), with the Midwest in second

I lunch at Wendy's, where $4.99 gets you unlimited refills at the Mexican part of the Superbar, a comforting surfeit of refried beans and "cheese sauce." A teenage employee, seeing me studying the want ads, kindly offers me an application form, which I fill out, though here, too, the pay is just $6 and change an hour. Then it's off for a round of the locally owned inns and guesthouses. At "The Palms," let's call it, a bouncy manager actually takes me around to see the rooms and meet the existing housekeepers, who, I note with-satisfaction, look pretty much like me—faded ex-hippie types in shorts with long hair pulled back in braids. Mostly, though, no one speaks to me or even looks at me except to proffer an application form. At my last stop, a palatial B & B, I wait twenty minutes to meet "Max," only to be told that there are no jobs now but there should be one soon, since "nobody lasts more than a couple weeks." (Because none of the people I talked to knew I was a reporter, I have changed their names to protect their privacy and, in some cases perhaps, their jobs.)

Three days go by like this, and, to my chagrin, no one out of the approximately twenty places I've applied calls me for an interview. I had been vain enough to worry about coming across as too educated for the jobs I sought, but no one even seems interested in finding out how overqualified I am. Only later will I realize that the want ads are not a reliable measure of the actual jobs available at any particular time. They are, as I should

---

place (50 percent). The drug mostly likely to be detected— marijuana, which can be detected in urine for weeks—is also the most innocuous, while heroine and cocaine are generally undetectable three days after use. Prospective employees sometimes try to cheat the tests by consuming excessive amounts of liquids and taking diuretics and even masking substances available through the Internet.

have guessed from Max's comment, the employers' insurance policy against the relentless turnover of the low-wage workforce. Most of the big hotels run ads almost continually, just to build a supply of applicants to replace the current workers as they drift away or are fired, so finding a job is just a matter of being at the right place at the right time and flexible enough to take whatever is being offered that day. This finally happens to me at one of the big discount hotel chains, where I go, as usual, for housekeeping and am sent, instead, to try out as a waitress at the attached "family restaurant," a dismal spot with a counter and about thirty tables that looks out on a garage and features such tempting fare as "Pollish [sic] sausage and BBQ sauce" on 95-degree days. Phillip, the dapper young West Indian who introduces himself as the manager, interviews me with about as much enthusiasm as if he were a clerk processing me for Medicare, the principal questions being what shifts can I work and when can I start. I mutter something about being woefully out of practice as a waitress, but he's already on to the uniform: I'm to show up tomorrow wearing black slacks and black shoes; he'll provide the rust-colored polo shirt with HEARTHSIDE embroidered on it, though I might want to wear my own shirt to get to work, ha ha. At the word "tomorrow," something between fear and indignation rises in my chest. I want to say, "Thank you for your time, sir, but this is just an experiment, you know, not my actual life."

So begins my career at the Hearthside, I shall call it, one small profit center within a global discount hotel chain, where for two weeks I work from 2:00 till 10:00 p.m. for $2.43 an hour plus tips.[3] In some futile bid for

---

3. According to the Fair Labor Standards Act, employers are

gentility, the management has barred employees from using the front door, so my first day I enter through the kitchen, where a red-faced man with shoulder-length blond hair is throwing frozen steaks against the wall and yelling, "Fuck this shit!" "That's just Jack," explains Gail, the wiry middle-aged waitress who is assigned to train me. "He's on the rag again"—a condition occasioned, in this instance, by the fact that the cook on the morning shift had forgotten to thaw out the steaks. For the next eight hours, I run after the agile Gail, absorbing bits of instruction along with fragments of personal tragedy. All food must be trayed, and the reason she's so tired today is that she woke up in a cold sweat thinking of her boyfriend, who killed himself recently in an upstate prison. No refills on lemonade. And the reason he was in prison is that a few DUIs caught up with him, that's all, could have happened to anyone. Carry the creamers to the table in a monkey bowl, never in your hand. And after he was gone she spent several months living in her truck, peeing in a plastic pee bottle and reading by candlelight at night, but you can't live in a truck in the summer, since you need to have the windows down, which means anything can get in, from mosquitoes on up.

At least Gail puts to rest any fears I had of appearing overqualified. From the first day on, I find that of all the things I have left behind, such as home and identity, what I miss the most is competence. Not that I have ever felt utterly competent in the writing business, in which

---

not required to pay "tipped employees," such as restaurant servers, more than $2.13 an hour in direct wages. However if the sum of the tips plus $2.13 an hour falls below the minimum wage, or $5.15 an hour, the employer is required to make up the difference. This fact was not mentioned by managers or otherwise publicized at either of the restaurants where I worked.

one day's success augurs nothing at all for the next. But in my writing life, I at least have some notion of procedure: do the research, make the outline, rough out a draft, etc. As a server, though, I am beset by requests like bees: more iced tea here, ketchup over there, a to-go box for table fourteen, and where are the high chairs, anyway? Of the twenty-seven tables, up to six are usually mine at any time, though on slow afternoons or if Gail is off, I sometimes have the whole place to myself. There is the touch-screen computer-ordering system to master, which is, I suppose, meant to minimize server-cook contact, but in practice requires constant verbal fine-tuning: "That's gravy on the mashed, okay? None on the meatloaf," and so forth—while the cook scowls as if I were inventing these refinements just to torment him. Plus, something I had forgotten in the years since I was eighteen: about a third of a server's job is "side work" that's invisible to customers—sweeping, scrubbing, slicing, refilling, and restocking. If it isn't all done, every little bit of it, you're going to face the 6:00 p.m. dinner rush defenseless and probably go down in flames. I screw up dozens of times at the beginning, sustained in my shame entirely by Gail's support—"It's okay, baby, everyone does that sometime"—because, to my total surprise and despite the scientific detachment I am doing my best to maintain, I care.

The whole thing would be a lot easier if I could just skate though it as Lily Tomlin in one of her waitress skits, but I was raised by the absurd Booker T. Washingtonian precept that says: If you're going to do something, do it well. In fact, "well" isn't good enough by half. Do it better than anyone has ever done it before. Or so said my father, who must have known what he was talking about because he managed to pull himself, and us with him, up from the mile-deep copper mines of Butte to the leafy suburbs of the Northeast, ascending from boiler-makers to martinis before booze beat out ambition. As in most endeavors I have encountered in my life, doing it "better than anyone" is not a reasonable goal. Still, when I wake up at 4:00 a.m. in my own cold sweat, I am not thinking about the writing deadlines I'm neglecting; I'm thinking about the table whose order I screwed up so that one of the boys didn't get his kiddie meal until the rest of the family had moved on to their Key Lime pies. That's the other powerful motivation I hadn't expected—the customers, or "patients," as I can't help thinking of them on account of the mysterious vulnera-bility that seems to have left them temporarily unable to feed themselves. After a few days at the Hearthside, I feel the service ethic kick in like a shot of oxytocin, the nurturance hormone. The plurality of my customers are hard-working locals—truck drivers, construction workers, even housekeepers from the attached hotel—and I want them to have the closest to a "fine dining" experience that the grubby circumstances will allow. No "you guys" for me; everyone over twelve is "sir" or "ma'am." I ply them with iced tea and coffee refills; I return, midmeal, to inquire how everything is; I doll up their salads with chopped raw mushrooms, summer squash slices, or whatever bits of produce I can find that have survived their sojourn in the cold-storage room mold-free.

There is Benny, for example, a short, tight-muscled sewer repairman, who cannot even think of eating until he has absorbed a half hour of air conditioning and ice water. We chat about hyperthermia and electrolytes until he is ready to order some finicky combination like soup of the day, garden salad, and a side of grits. There are the German tourists who are so touched by my pidgin "Willkommen" and "Ist alles gut?" that they actually tip.

(Europeans, spoiled by their trade-union-ridden, high-wage welfare states, generally do not know that they are supposed to tip. Some restaurants, the Hearthside included, allow servers to "grat" their foreign customers, or add a tip to the bill. Since this amount is added before the customers have a chance to tip or not tip, the practice amounts to an automatic penalty for imperfect English.) There are the two dirt-smudged lesbians, just off their construction shift, who are impressed enough by my suave handling of the fly in the piña colada that they take the time to praise me to Stu, the assistant manager. There's Sam, the kindly retired cop, who has to plug up his tracheotomy hole with one finger in order to force the cigarette smoke into his lungs.

Sometimes I play with the fantasy that I am a princess who, in penance for some tiny transgression, has undertaken to feed each of her subjects by hand. But the nonprincesses working with me are just as indulgent, even when this means flouting management rules—concerning, for example, the number of croutons that can go on a salad (six). "Put on all you want," Gail whispers, "as long as Stu isn't looking." She dips into her own tip money to buy biscuits and gravy for an out-of-work mechanic who's used up all his money on dental surgery, inspiring me to pick up the tab for his milk and pie. Maybe the same high levels of agape can be found throughout the "hospitality industry." I remember the poster decorating one of the apartments I looked at, which said "If you seek happiness for yourself you will never find it. Only when you seek happiness for others will it come to you," or words to that effect—an odd sentiment, it seemed to me at the time, to find in the dank one-room basement apartment of a bellhop at the Best Western. At the Hearthside, we utilize whatever bits of autonomy we have to ply our customers with the illicit calories that signal our love. It is our job as servers to assemble the salads and desserts, pouring the dressings and squirting the whipped cream. We also control the number of butter patties our customers get and the amount of sour cream on their baked potatoes. So if you wonder why Americans are so obese, consider the fact that waitresses both express their humanity and earn their tips through the covert distribution of fats.

Ten days into it, this is beginning to look like a livable lifestyle. I like Gail, who is "looking at fifty" but moves so fast she can alight in one place and then another without apparently being anywhere between them. I clown around with Lionel, the teenage Haitian busboy, and catch a few fragments of conversation with Joan, the svelte fortyish hostess and militant feminist who is the only one of us who dares to tell Jack to shut the fuck up. I even warm up to Jack when, on a slow night and to make up for a particularly unwarranted attack on my abilities, or so I imagine, he tells me about his glory days as a young man at "coronary school"—or do you say "culinary"?—in Brooklyn, where he dated a knock-out Puerto Rican chick and learned everything there is to know about food. I finish up at 10:00 or 10:30, depending on how much side work I've been able to get done during the shift, and cruise home to the tapes I snatched up at random when I left my real home—Marianne Faithfull, Tracy Chapman, Enigma, King Sunny Adé, the Violent Femmes—just drained enough for the music to set my cranium resonating but hardly dead. Midnight snack is Wheat Thins and Monterey Jack, accompanied by cheap white wine on ice and whatever AMC has to offer. To bed by 1:30 or 2:00, up at 9:00 or 10:00, read for an hour while my uniform whirls around in the landlord's washing machine, and then it's another eight hours spent following Mao's central instruction, as laid out in the Little Red Book, which was: Serve the people.

I could drift along like this, in some dreamy proletarian idyll, except for two things. One is management. If I have kept this subject on the margins thus far it is because I still flinch to think that I spent all those weeks under the surveillance of men (and later women) whose job it was to monitor my behavior for signs of sloth, theft, drug abuse, or worse. Not that managers and especially "assistant managers" in low-wage settings like this are exactly the class enemy. In the restaurant business, they are mostly former cooks or servers, still capable of pinch-hitting in the kitchen or on the floor, just as in hotels they are likely to be former clerks, and paid a salary of only about $400 a week. But everyone knows they have crossed over to the other side, which is, crudely put, corporate as opposed to human. Cooks want to prepare tasty meals; servers want to serve them graciously; but managers are there for only one reason—to make sure that money is made for some theoretical entity that exists far away in Chicago or New York, if a corporation can be said to have a physical existence at all. Reflecting on her career, Gail tells me ruefully that she had sworn, years ago, never to work for a corporation again, "They don't cut you no slack. You give and you give, and they take."

Managers can sit—for hours at a time if they want—but it's their job to see that no one else ever does, even when there's nothing to do, and this is why, for servers, slow times can be as exhausting as rushes. You start dragging out each little chore, because if the manager on duty catches you in an idle moment, he will give you something far nastier to do. So I wipe, I clean, I consolidate ketchup bottles and recheck the cheesecake supply, even tour the tables to make sure the customer evaluation forms are all standing perkily in their places—wondering all the time how many calories I burn in these strictly theatrical exercises. When, on a dead afternoon, Stu finds me glancing at a *USA Today* a customer has left behind, he assigns me to vacuum the entire floor with the broken vacuum cleaner that has a handle only two feet long, and the only way to do that without incurring orthopedic damage is to proceed from spot to spot on your knees.

On my first Friday at the Hearthside there is a "mandatory meeting for all restaurant employees," which I attend, eager for insight into our overall marketing strategy and the niche (your basic Ohio cuisine with a tropical twist?) we aim to inhabit. But there is no "we" at this meeting. Phillip, our top manager except for an occasional "consultant" sent out by corporate headquarters, opens it with a sneer: "The break room—it's disgusting. Butts in the ashtrays, newspapers lying around, crumbs." This windowless little room, which also houses the time clock for the entire hotel, is where we stash our bags and civilian clothes and take our half-hour meal breaks. But a break room is not a right, he tells us. It can be taken away. We should also know that the lockers in the break room and whatever is in them can be searched at any time. Then comes gossip; there has been gossip; gossip (which seems to mean employees talking among themselves) must stop. Off-duty employees are henceforth barred from eating at the restaurant, because "other servers gather around them and gossip." When Phillip has exhausted his agenda of rebukes, Joan complains about the condition of the ladies' room and I throw in my two bits about the vacuum cleaner. But I don't see any backup coming from my fellow servers, each of whom has subsided into her own personal funk; Gail, my role model, stares sorrow-fully at a point six inches from her nose. The meeting ends when Andy, one of the cooks, gets up, muttering about breaking up his day off for this almighty bullshit.

Just four days later we are suddenly summoned into the kitchen at 3:30 p.m., even though there are live tables on the floor. We all—about ten of us—stand around Phillip, who announces grimly that there has been a report of some "drug activity" on the night shift and that, as a result, we are now to be a "drug-free" workplace, meaning that all new hires will be tested, as will possibly current employees on a random basis. I am glad that this part of the kitchen is so dark, because I find myself blushing as hard as if I had been caught toking up in the ladies' room myself: I haven't been treated this way—lined up in the corridor, threatened with locker searches, peppered with carelessly aimed accusations—since junior high school. Back on the floor, Joan cracks, "Next they'll be telling us we can't have sex on the job." When I ask Stu what happened to inspire the crackdown, he just mutters about "management decisions" and takes the opportunity to upbraid Gail and me for being too generous with the rolls. From now on there's to be only one per customer, and it goes out with the dinner, not with the salad. He's also been riding the cooks, prompting Andy to come out of the kitchen and observe—with the serenity of a man whose customary implement is a butcher knife—that "Stu has a death wish today."

Later in the evening, the gossip crystallizes around the theory that Stu is himself the drug culprit, that he uses the restaurant phone to order up marijuana and sends one of the late servers out to fetch it for him. The server was caught, and she may have ratted Stu out or at least said enough to cast some suspicion on him, thus accounting for his pissy behavior. Who knows? Lionel, the busboy, entertains us for the rest of the shift by standing just behind Stu's back and sucking deliriously on an imaginary joint.

The other problem, in addition to the less-than-nurturing management style, is that this job shows no sign of being financially viable. You might imagine, from a comfortable distance, that people who live, year in and year out, on $6 to $10 an hour have discovered some survival stratagems unknown to the middle class. But no. It's not hard to get my coworkers to talk about their living situations, because housing, in almost every case, is the principal source of disruption in their lives, the first thing they fill you in on when they arrive for their shifts. After a week, I have compiled the following survey:

> Gail is sharing a room in a well-known downtown flophouse for which she and a roommate pay about $250 a week. Her roommate, a male friend, has begun hitting on her, driving her nuts, but the rent would be impossible alone.

> Claude, the Haitian cook, is desperate to get out of the two-room apartment he shares with his girlfriend and two other, unrelated, people. As far as I can determine, the other Haitian men (most of whom only speak Creole) live in similarly crowded situations.

> Annette, a twenty-year-old server who is six months pregnant and has been abandoned by her boyfriend, lives with her mother, a postal clerk.

Marianne and her boyfriend are paying $170 a week for a one-person trailer.

Jack, who is, at $10 an hour, the wealthiest of us, lives in the trailer he owns, paying only the $400-a-month lot fee.

The other white cook, Andy, lives on his dry-docked boat, which, as far as I can tell from his loving descriptions, can't be more than twenty feet long. He offers to take me out on it, once it's repaired, but the offer comes with inquiries as to my marital status, so I do not follow up on it.

Tina and her husband are paying $60 a night for a double room in a Days Inn. This is because they have no car and the Days Inn is within walking distance of the Hearthside. When Marianne, one of the breakfast servers, is tossed out of her trailer for subletting (which is against the trailer-park rules), she leaves her boyfriend and moves in with Tina and her husband.

Joan, who had fooled me with her numerous and tasteful outfits (hostesses wear their own clothes), lives in a van she parks behind a shopping center at night and showers in Tina's motel room. The clothes are from thrift shops.[4]

---

4. I could find no statistics on the number of employed people living in cars or vans, but according to the National Coalition for the Homeless's 1997 report "Myths and Facts About Homelessness," nearly one in five homeless people (in twenty-nine cities across the nation) is employed in a full- or part-time job.

It strikes me, in my middle-class solipsism, that there is gross improvidence in some of these arrangements. When Gail and I are wrapping silverware in napkins—the only task for which we are permitted to sit—she tells me she is thinking of escaping from her roommate by moving into the Days Inn herself. I am astounded: How can she even think of paying between $40 and $60 a day? But if I was afraid of sounding like a social worker, I come out just sounding like a fool. She squints at me in disbelief, "And where am I supposed to get a month's rent and a month's deposit for an apartment?" I'd been feeling pretty smug about my $500 efficiency, but of course it was made possible only by the $1,300 I had allotted myself for start-up costs when I began my low-wage life: $1,000 for the first month's rent and deposit, $100 for initial groceries and cash in my pocket, $200 stuffed away for emergencies. In poverty, as in certain propositions in physics, starting conditions are everything.

There are no secret economies that nourish the poor; on the contrary, there are a host of special costs. If you can't put up the two months' rent you need to secure an apartment, you end up paying through the nose for a room by the week. If you have only a room, with a hot plate at best, you can't save by cooking up huge lentil stews that can be frozen for the week ahead. You eat fast food, or the hot dogs and styrofoam cups of soup that can be microwaved in a convenience store. If you have no money for health insurance—and the Hearthside's niggardly plan kicks in only after three months—you go without routine care or prescription drugs and end up paying the price. Gail, for example, was fine until she ran out of money for estrogen pills. She is supposed to be on the company plan by now, but they claim to have lost her application form and need to begin the paperwork all over again. So she spends $9 per migraine pill to control the headaches she wouldn't have, she insists, if her estrogen supplements were covered. Similarly, Marianne's boyfriend lost his job as a roofer because he missed so much time after getting a cut on his foot for which he couldn't afford the prescribed antibiotic.

My own situation, when I sit down to assess it after two weeks of work, would not be much better if this were my actual life. The seductive thing about waitressing is that you don't have to wait for payday to feel a few bills in your pocket, and my tips usually cover meals and gas, plus something left over to stuff into the kitchen drawer I use as a bank. But as the tourist business slows in the summer heat, I sometimes leave work with only $20 in tips (the gross is higher, but servers share about 15 percent of their tips with the busboys and bartenders). With wages included, this amounts to about the minimum wage of $5.15 an hour. Although the sum in the drawer is piling up, at the present rate of accumulation it will be more than a hundred dollars short of my rent when the end of the month comes around. Nor can I see any expenses to cut. True, I haven't gone the lentil-stew route yet, but that's because I don't have a large cooking pot, pot holders, or a ladle to stir with (which cost about $30 at Kmart, less at thrift stores), not to mention onions, carrots, and the indispensable bay leaf. I do make my lunch almost every day—usually some slow-burning, high-protein combo like frozen chicken patties with melted cheese on top and canned pinto beans on the side. Dinner is at the Hearthside, which offers its employees a choice of BLT, fish sandwich, or hamburger for only $2. The burger lasts longest, especially if it's heaped with gut-puckering jalapenos, but by midnight my stomach is growling again. . . .

• • •

When I moved out of the trailer park, I gave the key to number 46 to Gail and arranged for my deposit to be transferred to her. She told me that Joan is still living in her van and that Stu had been fired from the Hearthside. . . .

In one month, I had earned approximately $1,040 and spent $517 on food, gas, toiletries, laundry, phone, and utilities. If I had remained in my $500 efficiency, I would have been able to pay the rent and have $22 left over (which is $78 less than the cash I had in my pocket at the start of the month). During this time I bought no clothing except for the required slacks and no prescription drugs or medical care (I did finally buy some vitamin B to compensate for the lack of vegetables in my diet). Perhaps I could have saved a little on food if I had gotten to a supermarket more often, instead of convenience stores, but it should be noted that I lost almost four pounds in four weeks, on a diet weighted heavily toward burgers and fries.

How former welfare recipients and single mothers will (and do) survive in the low-wage workforce, I cannot imagine. Maybe they will figure out how to condense their lives—including child-raising, laundry, romance, and meals—into the couple of hours between full-time jobs. Maybe they will take up residence in their vehicles, if they have one. All I know is that I couldn't hold two jobs and I couldn't make enough money to live on with one. And I had advantages unthinkable to many of the long-term poor—health, stamina, a working car, and no children to care for and support. Certainly nothing in my experience contradicts the conclusion of Kathryn Edin and Laura Lein, in their recent book *Making Ends Meet: How Single Mothers Survive Welfare and Low-Wage Work*, that low-wage work actually involves more hardship and deprivation than life at the mercy of the welfare state. In the coming months and years, economic conditions for the working poor are bound to worsen, even without the almost inevitable recession. As mentioned earlier, the influx of former welfare recipients into the low-skilled workforce will have a depressing effect on both wages and the number of jobs available. A general economic downturn will only enhance these effects, and the working poor will of course be facing it without the slight, but nonetheless often saving, protection of welfare as a backup.

The thinking behind welfare reform was that even the humblest jobs are morally uplifting and psychologically buoying. In reality they are likely to be fraught with insult and stress. But I did discover one redeeming feature of the most abject low-wage work—the camaraderie of people who are, in almost all cases, far too smart and funny and caring for the work they do and the wages they're paid. The hope, of course, is that someday these people will come to know what they're worth, and take appropriate action.

FOR DISCUSSION

1. Why does Ehrenreich alternate Gail's comments about how to tray food and refuse refills on lemonade with her revelations about her boyfriend's conviction and suicide in prison?

2. Why does Ehrenreich compare "the service ethic" to "a shot of oxytocin, the nurturance hormone"? (33) Why does Ehrenreich feel compelled to provide her customers with a "fine dining" experience? (33)

3. Why does Ehrenreich fantasize "that I am a princess who, in penance for some tiny transgression, has undertaken to feed each of her subjects by hand"? (34) How does giving people more food than they are technically entitled to become an expression of humanity for Ehrenreich and her fellow servers?

4. What are the "special costs" borne by the poor, according to Ehrenreich? (41) Why does she conclude that low-wage jobs "are likely to be fraught with insult and stress"? (44)

FOR FURTHER REFLECTION

1. What "appropriate action" do you think Ehrenreich might suggest that low-wage workers take when they "come to know what they're worth"? (44) How do you think low-wage workers should respond to being underpaid or treated poorly?

2. Do you agree that restaurant managers and other supervisors of low-wage workers tend to cross "over to the other side," becoming more identified with the corporation than with their employees? (36)

Joan Frank (1949–) was born in Phoenix, Arizona, and has lived in Hawaii, West Africa, Paris, and San Francisco. A writer, university teacher, and book reviewer, she attended the University of California, Berkeley and obtained an MFA from Warren Wilson College in Asheville, North Carolina. Frank is known for her precisely crafted prose and her astute and witty observations about contemporary life, particularly the relationships between men and women. She has won many awards including the Iowa Short Fiction Award and the Michigan Literary Fiction Award. Her major works include the novel *The Great Far Away* (2007), the essay collection *Desperate Women Need to Talk to You* (1994), and the short story collections *Boys Keep Being Born* (2001) and *In Envy Country* (2010).

Betting on Men

Carver hadn't arrived yet that morning. Carver was always a couple of hours late, unless he was up to something, as Malcolm liked to say—so Malcolm took the opportunity to stick his head inside Bridget's office door.

"I may as well give you some news you won't like." His eyes bulged, a light she'd learned to recognize. He had information that would bear on her.

"Oh?" Bridget's heart stiffened, though her face assumed its Casually Yet Responsibly Amused look. Formed in a stroke. *Never be caught out of character.*

"What's up?" Voice bright, brisk. *Please just go away.*

It was not yet eight in the morning. Bridget had mastered the habit of arriving early, because she knew Malcolm would trudge up the stairs and see her settled at her desk. Malcolm set great store by such habits— early arrival, crisp dressing, neat workspace—the whole Andrew Carnegie rigmarole. Malcolm noticed, kept track, never forgot. He bought motivational books and videotapes, titles like *Play to Win*. Wore a jacket and tie each day, never took lunch, carried a heavy black three-ring binder in which every element of his present and future were plotted. Bridget knew Malcolm took the binder with him on vacation. Bridget also knew (he found ways to let it drop) that Malcolm rose at four in the morning to meditate upon his goals, enter them into that binder. One day she'd found it open on his desk. On every other page, amid the appointments in Malcolm's neat, square print, she also saw—flipping forward, back-ward—these carefully copied lines:

What are the facts?
What do you think?
How do you know?

Below them, an apparent breakdown of Malcolm's waking hours:

.4 professional
.1 family
.1 exercise
.2 spiritual
.2 self-improvement

After she saw those pages Bridget stumbled back to her own desk, dazed. She'd felt then as though she and all the others in the building were made of Gumby clay, living in a Gumby world. Furniture, cars, food—the entire earth, the wretched and the royal, the infinite universe and its boiling suns—Gumby-stuff, spatulate and squishy. She'd rummaged in her drawer until she found a chocolate cookie, taken small, careful bites, cupping a hand to catch the crumbs. She chewed slowly. Dark, sandy sweetness melted along her teeth into the slick membrane of her mouth's inner walls, infusing butterfat, cocoa, sugar. A tiny sigh escaped her. Still chewing, she threw the crumbs into the far back of her mouth as if they were aspirin, stared damply out her office window onto the empty street below.

Optical-Consolidated made coatings and filters for eyeglass lenses and medical equipment (applications for car windshields, computer screens, paints, plastics), and business in the last few years had shifted to warp speed. The headquarters where Bridget worked had set up several more production plants around the state. Bridget knew nothing about window films and light-interference pigments, but she didn't need to. Checks poured in through the daily mail that Bridget stamped and photocopied and stuffed into a depository bag (zipped sturdy, click-locked with a key). She added them first on the calculator: rich, threshing sounds, totaled with a chewy flourish. Those checks added up to more money any single day than anyone who worked for Opti-Con—excepting Carver, the owner, who was a millionaire—would ever see in their lifetimes. It did strange things to you to see that much money every day. Bridget talked to herself about it. *Twenty round-the-world cruises. Five medical-school educations. Homes. Cars. Land, clothing, food.* Even so, the checks Bridget handled seemed unreal. Play money. (Though Carver's platinum Jaguar and Malcolm's espresso Mercedes stood real enough, sleek as small aircraft, gleaming in the parking lot amid the scuffed sedans and trucks.) In fact very little seemed real to Bridget during office hours except the gauzy light through her second-story window, the soft sounds of cars and trucks passing below, the low hum of the computer's hard drive, the degree of comfort in her lower womb relative to how recently she'd emptied her bladder. A nest of swallows had built itself near the outside corner of her window—a dozen of them actually, conical clay masses made of thousands of beak-sized scraps of dung-colored mud, wedged under the building's eaves. A perfect bird-sized hole punctured the crown of each like an amphora, a feather or sprig of straw drooping out. Early mornings in spring Bridget watched the birds jet back and forth in round wide arcs like those whirling swings at the fair: feeding babies, fortifying nests (bits of mud, pass after pass), a chorus of clickings and murmurings as they swooped. This would enchant Bridget—until a ragged commotion set up when the birds fought. The angry chatter exploding in a linear rush like a string of firecrackers, the compact bodies dive-bombing their rivals, the furious blur as warriors faced off, hovering midair—chastened her. All was not nice, in birdland.

Carver Hammond had been a young university dropout when he took over the modest operation, bequeathed by his retiring parents. Now Carver's gold-foil business card announced him Chief Executive Officer. Malcolm and Bridget had been recruited, with dozens of others, in rapid order. The situation began harmlessly enough.

They all do, at first.

"These are the file systems." The young woman who'd trained her had waved her hand like a quiz-show hostess toward wall after wall of cabinets. Bridget's heart had sunk through the floor as she'd nodded. Here was the great lie, the great dysfunction. *You had to pretend you liked it, and you had to pretend you cared.* All her life Bridget had managed to sell herself to jobs like these, sending ahead a resumé of useable skills like itemized portable attachments. In four years Bridget had connived a way of working at Opti-Con which dwelt on the surface of her own awareness, a rosy skin of apparent attentiveness that never betrayed the truth: that she could never, in any part of her, take business posturings seriously. That despite the cheery noise they made, neither she nor her coworkers cared if they ever saw each other again. That if a paycheck could be deposited to her bank without her having to leave home, she'd rig that in a blink. A lifetime of such jobs had distilled Bridget's thinking to the simplest of longings:

To be left alone.

To read under a tree, the Japanese maple in the yard behind her cottage, an in-law unit with window boxes. Bridget had rented all her days. When her father died everything was left to her stepmother, a peevish woman who'd loathed Bridget. Bridget fled home at seventeen, eked an AA equivalent at the local university, then knocked around, keeping afloat as salesclerk, typist, waitress, now administrative assistant—what the British call a *dog's body.* Three husbands had appeared in stately succession, each of whom she had duly assisted: from each she had either resigned, or been fired. Counterculture children all, a gardener, a carpenter, a café socialist. None had owned property, none had money. There was one grown stepson, a directory assistance operator up in Oregon. Bridget wondered why it had taken her so long to grasp that the marriage model itself was—God help her—another business to run.

When Carver made Malcolm Chief Financial Officer, Bridget had agreed to serve as Malcolm's assistant in exchange for a raise, and an office of her own. The private office freed her for the first time from the slave work of the front desk. And the extra money made it possible to save—perhaps enough, one day, for a down payment on a small mobile home. True, her office was directly beside Malcolm's, and true, a special door fed between the two rooms so Malcolm could stroll in at any time. To her relief, Malcolm kept that door closed.

In exchange, though, Bridget had to endure Malcolm's terrible habit.

Malcolm spent the days buttonholing employees with vicious gossip—mostly about Carver, whom he hated, but also about other employees. Lamenting to each that he was buried with difficult, exacting work, Malcolm made his rounds—Human Resources, Controller, Order Processing—plying these people with bilious rumors.

Employees quickly understood he took nourishment from the habit: lip-smacking *dolorosa*.

And this morning?

"There will be fireworks today," Malcolm intoned, staring at her. It was his No Good Can Come Of This look, and it contained unmistakable relish. Never in her life had Bridget known anyone to take such pleasure from doom mongering. Maybe it was kin to ambulance chasing.

"What exactly are you—what are *we*—expecting?" Bridget asked. The hatred and distrust between Malcolm Lowe and Carver Hammond had been racing along like black mold. Malcolm loathed his chief, Bridget knew, because Carver had inherited a nouveau riche adulthood—wore aloha shirts to work, joined expensive tennis clubs, took his wife to Paris for dinner. Like other wealthy men (Bridget had worked for two), Carver pored over every tiny charge on credit card bills with mulish suspicion. Malcolm, on the other hand, was from the deep South, progeny of a drunkard father and a mother who'd simply disappeared. Malcolm had done time in the army; worked as a salesman for prefab houses before hooking the Opti-Con job.

Now the two men were corporate officers with six-figure salaries, and Bridget was their *admin*, necessary and generic as a plumbing fixture. It amused Bridget she might actually have married the fellows she served, had she but played the game—worn seed-pearl chokers, gone to certain parties. In their youths Bridget and Carver might have crossed paths on the same campus. Carver would have been cutting classes to hurry to rehearsal of a blues band he'd started, stopping en route to hock his parents' stereo speakers. Bridget would be returning to her au pair job from the university's library carrel, books clutched to her pounding heart—having written a poem to the handsome young student she'd admired at an adjacent table. She'd left it there for him while he'd gone to the bathroom, then fled. Malcolm, meanwhile, would have been marching in stifling heat over Alabama dirt, bearing a sixty-pound pack and a rifle amid moving planks of other sweating men kitted up the same way, lifting their boots to the hoarse, rhythmic shouting of a superior officer. A few years later Malcolm would be standing at the check-in desk of a Holiday Inn, raincoat folded over a suitcase-toting forearm, the other arm pressing a copy of *Think Your Way to Fabulous Success* against his side.

But why, Bridget wondered, did Malcolm stay at Opti-Con if the very sight of Carver—his spiky hair and restless gray eyes, his stocky swagger, shoulder-clapping camaraderie, chewing food with his mouth open, interrupting again and again to insist on some embarrassingly specious point—why stay on as Malcolm did, if Carver infuriated him so?

For that matter, why did Bridget herself stay on?

It wasn't complicated. Opti-Con paid well. Better than any other work available to a woman with Bridget's unremarkable education—far better than teaching school, for example. It was late to train for anything new; training required time and money. And it cost such energy. All that theater, that *presenting*. The older Bridget got, the more difficult presenting became. Harder to suppress the urge to laugh at these blinkered little zealots. Their comic solemnity. Their meeting's—my God, their meetings. Their infernal, brainwashed *pep*. Admitting of no past, only the frantic present, waving the blueprints about. *Going forward*, they called it. Bridget shook her head. The child's obligation to attend school became an adult worklife that became, inevitably, an albatross that began to reek. Should she be ashamed for wishing only to read, to water geraniums? Wasn't that why people played lotteries?

As to Malcolm's reason for staying—Opti-Con was worth millions now. *Fortune* magazine listed it. Carver was on the screen, a *player*, having to enlist a battery of CPAs and lawyers to shield his income from rapacious taxes. He liked trying to get Ted Turner or Bill Gates on the phone, certain they would be pleased to hear his thoughts. Every few months he made Bridget send them little gifts (good cigars, fountain pens, grappa in cut-glass bottles) with roguish personal notes from him, and every few months had to be satisfied when Gates's or Turner's secretaries sent an icy thank-you back to Bridget.

When Malcolm left Opti-Con, Bridget saw, he wasn't about to do it with nothing in his hands besides the receding warmth of a firm handshake.

Carver—who'd wakened slowly to the fact that his quiet, hound-faced CFO actually despised his every breath, and planned to demand a cut—was now positioning his own cannons. Both men had hired attorneys. Both avoided one another in the halls. Each addressed Bridget with a curt message for the other, the way divorcing parents might address a child seated midway between them at a long table: *Tell your mother to pass the salt. Tell your father I suggest he obtain the salt by his own means.* Bridget soaked in a shallow bath every morning (poached front and back) to soften her nerves, a steaming washcloth over her face to steam out ill will. Driving off from her cottage fragrant and moist, thermal mug of strong coffee in the dashboard's plastic holder, she would listen to the classics station, feel momentarily soothed. Opti-Con headquartered in the countryside near dairy and livestock farms; each day as she drove Bridget could roam her eyes over green hills and pastures, gamboling calves, lambs. Flocks of starlings lifted and cascaded to

Sleeper, Awake or the *Pastorale,* and Bridget would sigh. *How lovely the wild mustard in the green fields.* But within minutes of arrival at the hangar-shaped plant her stomach would tighten, her shoulders start to harden into a sort of iron T-bar.

"He's pulled something," Malcolm said now, jerking his head toward their chief's still-locked office. "It marks the last straw."

As usual, Bridget fastened her innocent gaze to his, her cheeks and eyes and forehead coagulated into sympathetic attention. How else to respond? What would Malcolm do if he knew her thoughts—murderously weary, drained to the bone, bored to gibbering by his spiteful, old-womanish act? His Rasputin campaign, contaminating every day by scarcely eight in the morning. How often had Bridget wanted to plead *for God's sake, give it a rest.* How often had she burst from the building, stood heaving lungfuls of cool air—to replace all the breath sucked from her, those hours upon days upon years of listening, nodding, making inane gabble? Her head rang with noise, falsity. It built up over years, she thought. Like birdshit.

Can you believe what Carver's done now? Malcolm's voice, low and urgent. *Taking the whole place down with him this way? a faithful team like you and me?* It was sticky, that implied moment of intimate conjugality: *you and me.* Sticky as flypaper. Because no sooner had Malcolm left your office than he'd visit another worker down the hall, telling tales on *you* in there. Like the course of any poison, it had visible effect. Employees were forced to listen, to agree and agree. Soon they began to ache all over with an unredressed feeling, like a low-grade virus. They felt like sheep who'd let themselves—*baa-ing* obligingly—be herded and gouged and bled.

Oh, but how they needed that paycheck.

They walked around staring at one another in a vapor of toxic bewilderment.

Malcolm lowered his voice now. "Carver wants sole signatory approval of checks going out. This, on top of the extra audits and inventories. It's an insult to my office, and I won't have it," he said.

Again Bridget heard the sensual relish. It made her think of words like *impeachment, court-martial.*

Malcolm folded his arms. "I've seen an attorney who's advised me that I have a good case. And that everything Carver says to me now should be documented," he said with thick satisfaction.

"So if he tries to talk to me, I may have to ask you to take notes," he added, watching her.

Here it was, then. His trump.

"Ah," Bridget said, her mind shrieking, flinging itself bloodily against her skull as her face kept itself stretched into a blank moon of sympathy. "Notes."

"Think you can handle that?" His face telegraphed its odd mix of triumph, token solicitousness, stealthy curiosity. Malcolm liked measuring her reactions to his news, to gage the veracity of his own hunches. Of course Malcolm didn't really value Bridget's opinions, except as they confirmed his own. And of course Bridget lied like a pimp—with a sincerity that amazed even her. Bizarrely, Bridget found her sympathies malleable. She could turn a dial, lock on, absorb the world Malcolm wished to represent. Project it completely, speak its language. Reflect back wholesale his rendition of things. Worse, some part of her *wanted* Malcolm to feel validated, knowing perfectly well his projection was Gumby clay. Wanted him to find whatever in hell it was the poor fuck needed, though he made five times her salary and would kick her prone body aside to get it. Deep at her center, Bridget *wanted happiness* for this sad, twisted creature who was paid too much to do too little, who cultivated people's misfortunes the way others crochet, who counted his own wildly inadvertent good luck as the direct result of copying dime-store tenets from motivational speakers into a zippered black binder.

Worse still: when Carver cornered Bridget in a similar session of opinion-harvesting, she found herself warmly attending *his* every signal. *She wanted the same happiness for Carver.* Carver in his bermudas and flip-flops, his breezy *howareyou* not a question. Yet Carver also grinned, told jokes, brought strawberries, chocolate, flowers. Transparent condescensions to be sure, paving his road to Rome—but his eagerness, against all logic, touched you. Some part of Carver was still a vain boy, playing air guitar to impress girls at parties. That was the part Bridget rushed to reassure. Sometimes Bridget was afraid her surface-self had become so adept at this witless will-to-good it would finally swallow up her real self, like a sleeping bag turned inside out. What drove this reflex? Estrogen? Husband-helping? Bridget was forty-eight. *When did you get to stop doing this?*

Of the two in her office that minute—Malcolm leaning morosely against her doorframe, herself perched at the desk, hands laced with alert, phony attention—one would retire on a fat chunk of severance pay, and one would not. Retire: meaning no more 6 a.m. *dee-dee-dee-deep* alarm, dissolving cottony dreams. No more scrounging for a piece of stale bread and mottled apple in the fridge so you wouldn't spend money you didn't have on lunch. No more fishing in the black jungle of the closet for clothing that did not bind or scratch or make you look like one of those listless women pushing a cart down fluorescent K-Mart aisles. No entering the office burning-eyed at 7:50 a.m.— turning on copiers, starting coffee, trashing last night's junk faxes.

No more feeling your heart and stomach drop, to see Malcolm's baleful figure slowly mounting the stairs.

No more wincing at passing inmates, seeing them wince back.

No. Bridget was sentenced to work at jobs like this for the rest of her life, to make enough money to live. Answering to men like Malcolm, who trotted myths of themselves before them like religious effigies in processionals. She would have to pander and lie to men she pitied and deplored—for a barely sufficient wage. But Bridget had done it for so long that some part of her also still imagined—*why? why?*—that whatever she said to these men, whatever she did for them, might finally count. Add up. Gather some karmic reward. On her tombstone, perhaps? *She'd Like to Buy the World a Coke?*

"I'm a big girl, Malcolm, and this is part of my job." Bridget felt her face form its competent smile. A dangerous, precipitous edge of some sort was approaching. She must take special care now not to fall in.

She held the smile steady. She was surely losing her mind. "I guess I can do what I'm asked," she added, with warm huskiness. *You and me. You and me.*

She would do what she always did: Say yes to everything. Keep mentally bundled, let conflicts roll past far above her as if she were watching from the bottom of a clear lake: a bottle-colored ceiling where light played through its roiling surface. She bent over her own daily list. Call the landscaper. Wire money to the tax board. Cancel the contract for linen delivery, renew the bottled water contract. Deliver financial statements to the bank—the bank which was nervously floating millions to Opti-Con, based on the millions the place was attracting. Fantastic, this financing game, the betting it represented. Men betting on men: a wondrous cantilevered tower, greed multiplying on itself, metastasizing out and out into raw untried space. Yes, it was still a male bastion. Because the men craved this stuff like sex, craved the taste and smell. It stirred and spurred them. The bulletins, indicators. A cresting wave you rode. Magically coming into existence with the advent of the business day, magically ceasing at five o'clock Friday—though if big dollars were at stake the men would stay up all night, fly around the world, change diapers if need be. They were young, these grinning bankers who came around. Young but not looking well, with blue cheeks and white flesh that slumped a little over starchy collars. Their handshakes were strong enough to bring water to your eyes, their own eyes brightly hard. The words they spoke were also brightly hard. Sometimes their breath was bad. When she smiled and shook hands with the bankers, trying not to breathe the smell of their awful breath, Bridget thought of a scene in *The Magic Christian*, elegant financiers in suits and bowler hats wading into a tank of raw sewage to retrieve the dollar bills scattered over its surface.

She heard familiar voices rising.

Carver's shadow had flicked past her door, striding into Malcolm's office. Bridget heard their voices spark.

Oh, no. Here it comes.

In a moment Malcolm opened Bridget's private door. He didn't knock.

"Bridget, can you come in here, please."

Dear Lord. No time to think. Get up. Get up.

She seized her pad and pen, walked to the doorway between her office and Malcolm's, backed herself gingerly against its frame. Carver stood facing Malcolm's desk, arms folded, legs wide apart. Malcolm sat behind his desk with his hands in his lap and his head retracted at the neck, eyelids flicking. Both men were pale.

She held the notebook before her. looked from one to the other.

"I want a tape recorder," Bridget announced as she shoved her way past the heavy glass door into the tiny electronics store. It was the first such store she had spotted from her car. "For my office. On my company's credit card."

"Okay," nodded the saleswoman. She was a large, older matron whose box-shaped bottom swayed in tent-like pants. Her quick eyes studied Bridget's, made the mental leap: if the credit card is good, ask no questions.

"I want a good one. The kind that picks up voices nearby. The kind you don't have to bend down and yell into," Bridget said, her voice loud and trembling. The only other customer in the place, a woman with a gray ponytail and straw hat, looked up.

"Fine," agreed the matron, turning back around to bob from side to side toward the display case behind the sales counter.

"I want the batteries that go with it, loaded into it right here, please. And lots of extra batteries," commanded Bridget like a bank robber.

"Right-ee-o." The matron lifted down a machine the size of a lunch box. She placed it on the glass counter with a pack of batteries; excused herself to find more in the back room.

Bridget scanned the store. Lit plastic 7-Up signs crammed against reading lamps, radios, extension cords, CD storage cases, kiddie night-lights. A half-dozen televisions sat along shelves opposite her, one switched on, sound conveniently muted. It was tuned to a travel channel.

The gray-ponytailed woman resumed browsing the jostling oddities: clip-on book lights, coin sorters. A plastic trout lit up and sang when she pressed a button, mouth clacking open and shut. The expensive things, from which the tape recorder had been extracted, stashed on shelves behind the counter—more difficult to shoplift, Bridget guessed, her stomach taut. The late morning shone whitely through the front window, the rest of humanity at that hour meek and enchained at an office or classroom desk—misting produce or washing glasses or making beds. The heedless white morning pulsed into the store like a laughing crazy whore: the morning would be anybody's, for the moment, who could afford her.

Malcolm had announced to Carver, as Bridget stood in the doorway that morning like a trapped hostage: "My attorney has advised me that from here on out, anytime you talk to me, someone should be present to take notes."

Carver hadn't flinched from his wide-legged, arms-folded stance.

His mouth twitched at its corners, a perceptible sneer. With effort he reorganized his face to express long-suffering, restrained, ironic patience.

"Fine with me," he said evenly.

Carver would never express surprise, for that would be to admit imperfect control. He took on his pained-diplomat voice.

"But you know, Malcolm, what a shame this is. What a shame. If ever there were anything you needed to say, you know my office door is always open."

This was a lie. Carver's office door was sealed shut most of the time, because he was on the phone trying to sell the entire operation for two hundred fifty million dollars, and everyone knew it. Everyone pretended not to know it, to humor Carver and keep their jobs. The buyers appeared to be a consortium from Diamond County to the south: a half-dozen young men and one woman with severe, expensive haircuts, dressed in wrinkled black linen. Some wore wire-rim spectacles. They'd looked about twelve years old as they toured the place, staring at Bridget and the other middle-aged sheep grazing blankly in their offices along the upper and lower hallways. Carver's whiffing the big money was painful to see: he'd led the group around like a NASA director, gesturing. Already he planned his speaking tour. He'd keep a private jet, several homes in different countries, a few million in trust for each of his three highly irritable young children, Ariana, Joshua, and Zeke. Door open or closed, Carver was fused to the phone, brokering, bartering, bluffing. You could hear him if the door was open, interrupting people by loudly repeating a single phrase. *But what I'm saying/what I'm saying/what I'm saying is/you've got to/you've got to/you've got to.* Louder and louder, till the other speaker had to give up, let Carver speak. And because Carver was owner, because he had the money, no one—save his wife, a trust-fund heiress and the only other person on planet Earth in a position to do it—could tell him to go fuck himself.

Bridget scribbled as fast as her hand could go.

"You have specifically instructed an employee that all checks be routed for your signature," Malcolm said. "And you have overridden my express wishes against another round of inventories and audits."

"That is my right," Carver answered coolly. Bridget knew these activities prepared the company for a sale. She moved pen across paper faster.

"These are insults to my office and my responsibility," Malcolm said. "According to my attorney—"

Carver cut him off.

"As owner I have the right to call these shots. It has nothing to do with undermining—"

"That's your creation," Malcolm said.

"Malcolm, the money! There had to be a way for me to see what was going out!"

"Get it done then, Carver," Malcolm said quietly. "Get the place sold. You've marched your buyers through here often enough. People aren't stupid, and your pretending doesn't make them—"

Carver went a bit yellow.

"That is between my attorneys and me! I have the right to work on this in total privacy. I do not have to disclose it to you or anyone else unless I actually have—"

"That's one spin to put on it," Malcolm noted.

"Malcolm, Diamondhead has not offered yet! We are trying to come to an agreement. This is tough!"

"My understanding is you've made it tougher by doubling the asking price. What I'm saying," Malcolm added as Carver went paler still and opened his mouth, "is if Diamondhead is ready to go, why not get it over with?"

"I won't rush it," Carver said fiercely. "It's very difficult to focus when every day I come in and another maneuver has been made without my—"

"1 think you're pointing the finger in the wrong direction," Malcolm said. "There should be an atmosphere of trust here. People just want to come and do their work and go home. Right now," he said, "they feel like meat in a butcher's display case."

Bridget felt a force field expanding from Malcolm's desk like a hot, clear balloon. She wanted to cover her ears.

"These are not simple documents. There's a lot at stake," Carver said.

Boy, *was* there, she thought. But only one man would collect those spoils, and they all knew it. They also knew that Opti-Con had flourished despite Carver, never because of him. He gave useless orders; squandered money on limousines, spas, air-ionizers; bragged, complained, offended people. He was the founder's son.

"I'm trying like hell to resolve this," Carver was saying. "And *I'm trying to take you with me, Malcolm.*"

Carver inflected this the way parents spell c-a-n-d-y in front of a toddler. He gazed meaningfully at Malcolm.

Ho, thought Bridget as she scribbled. *Take this purse filled with gold for your troubles, my good man.* Here was Malcolm's off-ramp.

"All I'm asking is you do your job," Carver continued, softly now.

"I made a mistake with the checks. But I'm coming off this charged atmosphere. These incendiary stories. You have turned my employees against me, Malcolm. There is a trail of ugly stories I follow and it leads back to Malcolm Lowe.

"You've even turned Bridget against me," he said, his chin thrusting up.

Malcolm's eyebrows lifted a notch. Both men turned to look at her.

Bridget's writing stopped. A bolt shot through her.

"Have I done that, Bridget?" Malcolm asked.

Bridget threw her eyes out the window. Morning light swathed the street. A school bus trundled past, and a pickup truck piled with green blocks of hay. Two dogs pranced smiling, followed by an elderly couple. A young woman pushed a stroller. Men and women and children, calm, unafflicted, living their lives apart from this antler-lock caging her. Lives concerned with honorable trivia. Groceries, lawns, mail.

"Listen," Bridget began. Her mucousy throat gurgled the word. She cleared it strenuously.

"Listen, you guys, this can't be about me! I only want to do my work and not be put in anybody's camp. That's all I want, I swear." Her face burned.

Malcolm, pleased with this vague echo of his party line, looked back to Carver, who stood, arms folded, legs apart—the way Superman stands when ordinary mortals try shooting at him with ordinary bullets.

"Of course you do," Carver snarled at Bridget.

Abruptly he turned back to Malcolm. The rest of the staff were toilet paper, but Malcolm ran the numbers. Carver spoke with something close to tenderness.

"Malcolm, I agree this is nonsense. Believe me, I want it over as much as you."

"We're all anxious for resolution," Malcolm sniffed.

Bridget noted the *we*. What *we*, she wondered.

"One baby step at a time," Carver crooned. "Have lunch with me today, Malcolm. We'll hammer at it."

He means, thought Bridget, hammer it out.

Bridget leaned heavily against the glass countertop.

She let her eyes do the easy thing—drift to the television screen.

The travel channel camera panned over a harbor, perhaps Burma, somewhere steaming and green and very poor, a grimy harbor rusting with old cargo liners. Then the camera moved out from the harbor, the water sewer brown. A small barque came in view, pushed by a young man in rags. He worked the boat's pushing pole with a foot, one arm clinging to the craft's makeshift mast; the other dragged a fishing net. His movements were lopsided, automatic, well practiced.

Then the scene changed: a building project on a wet mountainside. Narrow terraces were being cut; along these, skinny workers covered in mud moved rocks and boulders off to a pile. Perhaps they were making a road. The camera zoomed in on the men's bare legs and feet, placed carefully on mud as they hauled the stones, balancing loads on heads or shoulders, dumping them finally off a shallow embankment. The men's faces wore an impenetrable fatalism. Some were boys. All sharply thin, smeared with sweat, yellow-brown mud. A harried busyness about the masses of them, including those who seemed to boss them. All evinced little thought other than to keep the sodden mess moving, rippling and staggering the cargo along in their bare hands the way crumbs of food are moved by ants.

Bridget's knees trembled. Her stomach twisted on itself: she pressed it harder against the counter. She wanted to fly out of the store into the harsh white sky, shamed to the soles of her feet. Her feet! Smooth and clean and pinkly nourished, feet that only went bare when she swam or bathed, padded on cool lawns in a suburban yard or park. She wanted to go back to the Opti-Con office and take the two men by their collars, drag them the length of the highway to the airport. Stuff them into a cargo carrier; fly them to the Burmese building site. Strip them to their shorts. Away with the thick wallets, the glistening Rolexes, the heavy gold rings, away with the keys to the silver Jag and espresso Mercedes, the Italian shoes, the zippered three-ring binder, the Palm Pilot, the Diet Cokes, moisturizing face spray. Prod them forward into the mud-splashed, empty-faced, milling lines of stone carriers. Carver and Malcolm would carry boulders and branches and sticky detritus of wet, steaming earth from earliest light until dark, when they would be given a small bowl of white rice. They would sleep on a mat of woven reeds if they were lucky, otherwise they would sleep on the mud itself. Mud they would be forced to excavate, live in, breathe and eat and shit in and be coated with, mud that would grind deeply into every pore and crevice of them, their anuses, pubic hair, their ears, each of their torn fingernails and splitting toenails, their eyes and scalps and mouths and down their throats, cover them for the rest of their wretched and pointless and queerly abbreviated lives.

Mud that would never, ever wash away.

"Thank you," Bridget croaked to the saleswoman who'd placed in Bridget's hands the brown plastic bag, weighty with the expensive machine inside, the machine loaded, poised to record the human voice. The plastic bag crinkled importantly. Bridget took a last look at the silent television. Swarms of thin men and boys struggled, with resigned vacantness, against the sopping earth. Holding her package from underneath with both hands, Bridget found her way to the shop's door, began to shoulder through. As she emerged her eyes floated up without purpose, so that quite by accident they caught sight of the eaves under the little store's roof.

She saw the swallows' nests, and remembered.

Tiny. Tireless. Ferociously building their hivelike fortresses, back and forth, with mud. Bits upon bits, pass after pass. Heedless persistence. Hierarchies of power, space. Sudden avalanches of chatter: furious, symphonic fights. Disappearing in afternoon to sleep, so they could begin it all again.

All was not nice, in birdland.

There was a curious calm in it, if you relinquished feeling you had to personally account for it. If you gave up the fraying hope that it not end badly, you got back something. Something that placed you again in the present, rolled the odometer back to zero, let you recommence making your way. Why this was so, she couldn't immediately say. But it was. Slowly, Bridget stepped clear of the store's entrance, let go of the opened door. Blinking, looking about, she walked into the whitely lit noon; walked from one world back into that from which she'd come, into the given day with her burden.

FOR DISCUSSION

1. When Bridget is first shown the office files, why does she think "the great lie, the great dysfunction" is that *you had to pretend you liked it, and you had to pretend you cared*"? (50)

2. Why does Bridget think the hours she has spent listening to Malcolm and hiding her feelings have built up over the years "like birdshit"? (55)

3. Why does Bridget think of the bank's loans to Opti-Con as "men betting on men"? (59)

4. Why is Bridget "shamed to the soles of her feet" by the images she sees on the television screen in the electronics store? (66)

FOR FURTHER REFLECTION

1. To what extent is Bridget a victim of others, and to what extent does she create her own problems?

2. Is it possible to work without engaging in "the great lie" Bridget describes? (50) How might someone keep his or her "real self" alive while doing work that is unfulfilling?

David Sedaris (1956–) grew up in North Carolina. After dropping out of Kent State University and hitchhiking around the United States, he moved to Chicago, and in 1987 he earned a degree from the School of the Art Institute of Chicago. He also performed readings from his diaries at local clubs and, eventually, on Chicago's public radio station. In 1991 Sedaris moved to New York and was invited to perform "SantaLand Diaries" on National Public Radio. This appearance catapulted him into the spotlight and cemented his reputation as a storyteller. Sedaris is known for his humorous, often satirical writing, which frequently draws on his odd experiences growing up and on his various day jobs, including working as a house cleaner. Sedaris's best-selling collections include *Barrel Fever* (1994), which features "SantaLand Diaries"; *Naked* (1997); *Me Talk Pretty One Day* (2000); and *Dress Your Family in Corduroy and Denim* (2004).

SantaLand Diaries
(selection)

I was in a coffee shop looking through the want ads when I read, "Macy's Herald Square, the largest store in the world, has big opportunities for outgoing, fun-loving people of all shapes and sizes who want more than just a holiday job! Working as an elf in Macy's SantaLand means being at the center of the excitement. . . ."

I circled the ad and then I laughed out loud at the thought of it. The man seated next to me turned on his stool, checking to see if I was a lunatic. I continued to laugh, quietly. Yesterday I applied for a job at UPS. They are hiring drivers' helpers for the upcoming Christmas season and I went to their headquarters filled with hope. In line with three hundered other men and women my hope diminished. During the brief interview I was asked why I wanted to work for UPS and I answered that I wanted to work for UPS because I like the brown uniforms. What did they expect me to say?

"I'd like to work for UPS because, in my opinion, it's an opportunity to showcase my substantial leadership skills in one of the finest private delivery companies this country has seen since the Pony Express!"

I said I liked the uniforms and the UPS interviewer turned my application facedown on his desk and said, "Give me a break."

I came home this afternoon and checked the machine for a message from UPS but the only message I got was from the company that holds my student loan, Sallie Mae. Sallie Mae sounds like a naive and barefoot hillbilly girl but in fact they are a ruthless and aggressive conglomeration of bullies located in a tall brick building somewhere in Kansas. I picture it to be the tallest building in that state and I have decided they hire their employees straight out of prison. It scares me.

The woman at Macy's asked, "Would you be interested in full-time elf or evening and weekend elf?"

I said, "Full-time elf."

I have an appointment next Wednesday at noon.

I am a thirty-three-year-old man applying for a job as an elf.

I often see people on the streets dressed as objects and handing out leaflets. I tend to avoid leaflets but it breaks my heart to see a grown man dressed as a taco. So, if there is a costume involved, I tend not only to accept the leaflet, but to accept it graciously, saying, "Thank you so much," and thinking, *You poor, pathetic son of a bitch. I don't know what you have but I hope I never catch it.* This afternoon on Lexington Avenue I accepted a leaflet from a man dressed as a camcorder. Hot dogs, peanuts, tacos, video cameras, these things make me sad because they don't fit in on the streets. In a parade, maybe, but not on the streets. I figure that at least as an elf I will have a place; I'll be in Santa's Village with all the other elves. We will reside in a fluffy wonderland surrounded by candy canes and gingerbread shacks. It won't be quite as sad as standing on some street corner dressed as a french fry.

I am trying to look on the bright side. I arrived in New York three weeks ago with high hopes, hopes that have been challenged. In my imagination I'd go straight from Penn Station to the offices of *One Life to Live*, where I would drop off my bags and spruce up before heading off for drinks with Cord Roberts and Victoria Buchannon, the show's greatest stars. We'd sit in a plush booth at a tony cocktail lounge where my new celebrity friends would lift their frosty glasses in my direction and say, "A toast to David Sedaris, the best writer this show has ever had!!!"

I'd say, "You guys, cut it out." It was my plan to act modest.

People at surrounding tables would stare at us, whispering, "Isn't that . . . ? Isn't that . . . ?"

I might be distracted by their enthusiasm and Victoria Buchannon would lay her hand over mine and tell me that I'd better get used to being the center of attention.

But instead I am applying for a job as an elf. Even worse than applying is the very real possibility that I will not be hired, that I couldn't even find work as an elf. That's when you know you're a failure.

This afternoon I sat in the eighth-floor SantaLand office and was told, "Congratulations, Mr. Sedaris. You are an elf."

In order to become an elf I filled out ten pages' worth of forms, took a multiple-choice personality test, underwent two interviews, and submitted urine for a drug test. The first interview was general, designed to eliminate the obvious sociopaths. During the second interview we were asked why we wanted to be elves. This is always a problem question. I listened as the woman ahead of me, a former waitress, answered the question, saying, "I really want to be an elf? Because I think it's about acting? And before this I worked in a restaurant? Which was run by this really wonderful woman who had a dream to open a restaurant? And it made me realize that it's really really . . . important to have a . . . dream?"

Everything this woman said, every phrase and sentence, was punctuated with a question mark and the interviewer never raised an eyebrow.

When it was my turn I explained that I wanted to be an elf because it was one of the most frightening career opportunities I had ever come across. The interviewer raised her face from my application and said, "And. . . ?"

I'm certain that I failed my drug test. My urine had roaches and stems floating in it, but still they hired me because I am short, five feet five inches. Almost everyone they hired is short. One is a dwarf. After the second interview I was brought to the manager's office, where I was shown a floor plan. On a busy day twenty-two thousand people come to visit Santa, and I was told that it is an elf's lot to remain merry in the face of torment and adversity. I promised to keep that in mind.

I spent my eight-hour day with fifty elves and one perky, well-meaning instructor in an enormous Macy's classroom, the walls of which were lined with NCR 2152s. A 2152, I have come to understand, is a cash register. The class was broken up into study groups and given assignments. My group included several returning elves and a few experienced cashiers who tried helping me by saying things like, "Don't you even know your personal ID code? Jesus, I had mine memorized by ten o'clock."

Everything about the cash register intimidates me. Each procedure involves a series of codes: separate numbers for cash, checks, and each type of credit card. The term *Void* has gained prominence as the filthiest four-letter word in my vocabulary. Voids are a nightmare of paperwork and coded numbers, everything produced in triplicate and initialed by the employee and his supervisor.

Leaving the building tonight I could not shake the mental picture of myself being stoned to death by restless, angry customers, their nerves shattered by my complete lack of skill. I tell myself that I will simply pry open my register and accept anything they want to give me—beads, cash, watches, whatever. I'll negotiate and swap. I'll stomp their credit cards through the masher, write "Nice Knowing You!" along the bottom of the slip, and leave it at that.

All we sell in SantaLand are photos. People sit upon Santa's lap and pose for a picture. The Photo Elf hands them a slip of paper with a number printed along the top. The form is filled out by another elf and the picture arrives by mail weeks later. So really, all we sell is the idea of a picture. One idea costs nine dollars, three ideas cost eighteen.

My worst nightmare involves twenty-two thousand people a day standing before my register. I won't always be a cashier, just once in a while. The worst part is that after I have accumulated three hundred dollars I have to remove two hundred, fill out half a dozen forms, and run the envelope of cash to the drop in the China Department or to the vault on the balcony above the first floor. I am not allowed to change my clothes beforehand. I have to go dressed as an elf. An elf in SantaLand is one thing, an elf in Sportswear is something else altogether.

This afternoon we were given presentations and speeches in a windowless conference room crowded with desks and plastic chairs. We were told that during the second week of December, SantaLand is host to "Operation Special Children," at which time poor children receive free gifts donated by the store. There is another morning set aside for terribly sick and deformed children. On that day it is an elf's job to greet the child at the Magic Tree and jog back to the house to brace our Santa.

"The next one is missing a nose," or "Crystal has third-degree burns covering 90 percent of her body."

Missing a nose. With these children Santa has to be careful not to ask, "And what would *you* like for Christmas?"

We were given a lecture by the chief of security, who told us that Macy's Herald Square suffers millions of dollars' worth of employee theft per year. As a result the store treats its employees the way one might treat a felon with a long criminal record. Cash rewards are offered for turning people in and our bags are searched every time we leave the store. We were shown videotapes in which supposed former employees hang their head and rue the day they ever thought to steal that leather jacket. The actors faced the camera to explain how their arrests had ruined their friendships, family life, and, ultimately, their future.

One fellow stared at his hands and sighed, "There's no way I'm going to be admitted into law school. Not now. Not after what I've done. Nope, no way." He paused and shook his head of the unpleasant memory. "Oh, man, not after this. No way."

A lonely, reflective girl sat in a coffee shop, considered her empty cup, and moaned, "I remember going out after work with all my Macy's friends. God, those were good times. I loved those people." She stared off into space for a few moments before continuing, "Well, needless to say, those friends aren't calling anymore. This time I've *really* messed up. Why did I do it? Why?"

Macy's has two jail cells on the balcony floor and it apprehends three thousand shoplifters a year. We were told to keep an eye out for pickpockets in SantaLand.

· · ·

Interpreters for the deaf came and taught us to sign, "MERRY CHRISTMAS! I AM SANTA'S HELPER." They told us to speak as we sign and to use bold, clear voices and bright facial expressions. They taught us to say, "YOU ARE A VERY PRETTY BOY/GIRL! I LOVE YOU! DO YOU WANT A SURPRISE?"

My sister Amy lives above a deaf girl and has learned quite a bit of sign language. She taught some to me and so now I am able to say, "SANTA HAS A TUMOR IN HIS HEAD THE SIZE OF AN OLIVE. MAYBE IT WILL GO AWAY TOMORROW BUT I DON'T THINK SO."

This morning we were lectured by the SantaLand managers and presented with a Xeroxed booklet of regulations titled *The Elfin Guide*. Most of the managers are former elves who have worked their way up the candy-cane ladder but retain vivid memories of their days in uniform. They closed the meeting saying, "I want you to remember that even if you are assigned Photo Elf on a busy weekend, YOU ARE NOT SANTA'S SLAVE."

In the afternoon we were given a tour of SantaLand, which really is something. It's beautiful, a real wonderland, with ten thousand sparkling lights, false snow, train sets, bridges, decorated trees, mechanical penguins and bears, and really tall candy canes. One enters and travels through a maze, a path which takes you from one festive environment to another. The path ends at the Magic Tree. The Tree is supposed to resemble a complex system of roots, but looks instead like a scale model of the human intestinal tract. Once you pass the Magic Tree, the light dims and an elf guides you to Santa's house. The houses are cozy and intimate, laden with toys. You exit Santa's house and are met with a line of cash registers.

We traveled the path a second time and were given the code names for various posts, such as "The Vomit

Corner," a mirrored wall near the Magic Tree, where nauseous children tend to surrender the contents of their stomachs. When someone vomits, the nearest elf is supposed to yell "VAMOOSE," which is the name of the janitorial product used by the store. We were taken to the "Oh, My God, Corner," a position near the escalator. People arriving see the long line and say "Oh, my God!" and it is an elf's job to calm them down and explain that it will take no longer than an hour to see Santa.

On any given day you can be an Entrance Elf, a Water Cooler Elf, a Bridge Elf, Train Elf, Maze Elf, Island Elf, Magic Window Elf, Emergency Exit Elf, Counter Elf, Magic Tree Elf, Pointer Elf, Santa Elf, Photo Elf, Usher Elf, Cash Register Elf, Runner Elf, or Exit Elf. We were given a demonstration of the various positions in action, performed by returning elves who were so animated and relentlessly cheerful that it embarrassed me to walk past them. I don't know that I could look someone in the eye and exclaim, "Oh, my goodness, I think I see Santa!" or "Can you close your eyes and make a very special Christmas wish!" Everything these elves said had an exclamation point at the end of it!!! It makes one's mouth hurt to speak with such forced merriment. I feel cornered when someone talks to me this way. Doesn't everyone? I prefer being frank with children. I'm more likely to say, "You must be exhausted," or "I know a lot of people who would kill for that little waistline of yours."

I am afraid I won't be able to provide the grinding enthusiasm Santa is asking for. I think I'll be a low-key sort of an elf.

Today was elf dress rehearsal. The lockers and dressing rooms are located on the eighth floor, directly behind SantaLand. Elves have gotten to know one another over the past four days of training but once we took off our clothes and put on the uniforms everything changed.

The woman in charge of costuming assigned us our outfits and gave us a lecture on keeping things clean. She held up a calendar and said. "Ladies, you know what this is. Use it. I have scraped enough blood out from the crotches of elf knickers to last me the rest of my life. And don't tell me, 'I don't wear underpants, I'm a dancer.' You're not a dancer. If you were a real dancer you wouldn't be here. You're an elf and you're going to wear panties like an elf."

My costume is green. I wear green velvet knickers, a yellow turtleneck, a forest-green velvet smock, and a perky stocking cap decorated with spangles. This is my work uniform.

My elf name is Crumpet. We were allowed to choose our own names and given permission to change them according to our outlook on the snowy world.

Today was the official opening day of SantaLand and I worked as a Magic Window Elf, a Santa Elf, and an Usher Elf. The Magic Window is located in the adult "Quick Peep" line. My job was to say, "Step on the Magic Star and look through the window, and you can see Santa!" I was at the Magic Window for fifteen minutes before a man approached me and said, "You look so fucking stupid."

I have to admit that he had a point. But still, I wanted to say that at least I get paid to look stupid, that he gives it away for free. But I can't say things like that because I'm supposed to be merry.

So instead I said, "Thank you!"

"Thank you!" as if I had misunderstood and thought he had said, "You look terrific."

"Thank you!"

He was a brawny wise guy wearing a vinyl jacket and carrying a bag from Radio Shack. I should have said, real loud, "Sorry, man, I don't date other guys." . . .

I spent a few hours in the Maze with Puff, a young elf from Brooklyn. We were standing near the Lollipop Forest when we realized that *Santa* is an anagram of *Satan*. Father Christmas or the Devil—so close but yet so far. We imagined a SatanLand where visitors would wade through steaming pools of human blood and feces before arriving at the Gates of Hell, where a hideous imp in a singed velvet costume would take them by the hand and lead them toward Satan. Once we thought of it we couldn't get it out of our minds. Overhearing the customers we would substitute the word *Satan* for the word *Santa*.

"What do you think, Michael? Do you think Macy's has the real Satan?"

"Don't forget to thank Satan for the Baby Alive he gave you last year."

"I love Satan."

"Who doesn't? Everyone loves Satan." . . .

This was my last day of work. We had been told that Christmas Eve is a slow day, but this was the day a week of training was meant to prepare us for. It was a day of nonstop action, a day when the managers spent a great deal of time with their walkie-talkies.

I witnessed a fistfight between two mothers and watched while a woman experienced a severe, crowd-related anxiety attack: falling to the floor and groping for breath, her arms moving as though she were fighting off bats. A Long Island father called Santa a faggot because he couldn't take the time to recite "The Night

Before Christmas" to his child. Parents in long lines
disposable diapers at the door to Santa's house. It wa
rowdiest crowd I have ever seen, and we were short on
elves, many of whom simply did not show up or called
in sick. As a result we had our lunch hours cut in half
and had to go without our afternoon breaks. Many elves
complained bitterly, but the rest of us found ourselves
in the moment we had all been waiting for. It was us
against them. It was time to be a trouper, and I surrendered completely. My Santa and I had them on the lap,
off the lap in forty-five seconds flat. We were an efficient
machine surrounded by chaos. Quitting time came and
went for the both of us and we paid it no mind. My
plane was due to leave at eight o'clock, and I stayed until
the last moment, figuring the time it would take to get
to the airport. It was with reservation that I reported to
the manager, telling her I had to leave. She was at a cash
register, screaming at a customer. She was, in fact, calling
this customer a bitch. I touched her arm and said, "I have
to go now." She laid her hand on my shoulder, squeezed
it gently, and continued her conversation, saying, "Don't
tell the store president I called you a bitch. Tell him I
called you a fucking bitch, because that's exactly what
you are. Now get out of my sight before I do something
we both regret."

FOR DISCUSSION

1. Why does Sedaris describe the economic realities and sometimes rude behavior of customers and workers in SantaLand but also say it is "beautiful, a real wonderland"? (77)

2. Why does Sedaris feel embarrassed to walk by the "animated and relentlessly cheerful" returning elves? (78)

3. Why do Sedaris and his coworker imagine "SatanLand"? (80)

4. Why does Sedaris take pleasure in being "an efficient machine surrounded by chaos"? (81)

FOR FURTHER REFLECTION

1. Who or what is the primary object of the satire in "SantaLand Diaries"?

2. Does Sedaris's scorn for aspects of working in SantaLand seem warranted or is it an overreaction?

Po Bronson (1964–) was born in Seattle and attended Stanford University (BA) and San Francisco State University (MFA). He worked for two years as a bond salesman, which provided the material for his first novel, *Bombardiers* (1995), a satirical look at high finance. Both as a novelist and a narrative nonfiction journalist, Bronson is known for thoroughly immersing himself in the world of his subjects. For his second novel, *The First $20 Million Is Always The Hardest* (1997), Bronson spent two years in California's Silicon Valley, observing the movers and shakers in the information technology revolution, a world he returned to again in his nonfiction work *The Nudist on the Late Shift and Other True Tales of Silicon Valley* (1999), from which "The Entrepreneur" is taken. In *What Should I Do With My Life?* (2003), Bronson documents the lives of ordinary people who make unusual career changes. Bronson is the cofounder of the Writers' Grotto, a writing cooperative in San Francisco.

The Entrepreneur

From the moment I met him, Sabeer Bhatia has given credit to the power of the idea. The idea was so powerful that when his friend and coworker Jack Smith, who was driving home to Livermore across the Dunbarton Bridge, called Sabeer on his car phone to brainstorm the pregnant thought that had just occurred to him, Sabeer heard one sentence of it and said, "Oh, my! Hang up that cellular and call me back on a secure line when you get to your house! We don't want anyone to overhear!"

It was so powerful an idea that when Jack did call Sabeer back fifteen minutes later, their minds melded as they talked, completely in sync, leaping from one ramification to the next as simultaneously as the steps of two soldiers marching side by side. It was so powerful that sleep that night was impossible for Sabeer, with the idea now in his head, exploding, autocatalytic, a bonfire of the mind. He stayed up all night, sitting at the glass-topped dining table in his small Bayside Village apartment, writing the business plan, which he took to his day job the next morning, looking so haggard that his boss stopped him and said, "You've got to cut out the partying, Sabeer." Sabeer—afraid the idea might pop out of his mouth if he opened it at all—just nodded. He was afraid even to make a single photocopy of the plan he had printed out, lest a stray page find its way into the recycling bin and then under someone else's gaze.

The idea came about this way: Sabeer and Jack had wanted to start a company, and they had been brainstorming possible business ideas for a few months. They wanted to e-mail each other notes, but they had been afraid that their bosses might glean their e-mail and accuse them of spending their working hours on personal projects (an accurate accusation). The budding entrepreneurs had personal America Online accounts, but these couldn't be accessed through the office network. On the evening he was driving home across the Dunbarton Bridge, Jack Smith had been frustrated all day by this problem. Then it occurred to him:

Free e-mail accounts that can be accessed anonymously, over the web.

In getting over their own obstacle to coming up with a business idea, they came up with just that idea.

It was an idea that had been lurking under the nose of every budding entrepreneur in the world. Any disgruntled employee who had ever worried about an employer reading his e-mail *could* have had the idea before Jack and Sabeer. *Anyone* could have had the idea. *You* could have had the idea. *I* could have had the idea.

It was the kind of idea that inspires legions of entrepreneurs. It was the kind of idea that spurs thousands of young people to give up their lives elsewhere and crash the Valley party. It sent the message and cc'd the entire world: to make it in Silicon Valley, you just have to come up with the right idea. You don't have to know the right people. You don't have to demonstrate experience. Most importantly, in this new era of the Internet, to come up with a good idea you don't have to be an *über*-geek who understands fiber-optic switching and site mirroring and massively parallel processing. It was as if a great wave had broken. For two decades, the science of technology had grown exponentially more sophisticated, and the cutting edge of technology was being shaped by those with PhDs from MIT and a dozen patents to their name, the kind of deep brainiacs who scare the media elite into thinking that the future will be dominated by Birkenstock-wearing coders with poor sartorial taste. High tech was becoming harder to understand for the casual observer; it was all about 32-bit versus 64-bit chipsets and low-earth-orbit satellite routing and 3-D vector-based graphics. The East Coast establishment was getting very uneasy, in the mid-1990s, as they woke up in the morning to the fear that having a law degree from Yale or an MBA from Wharton was no longer a guarantee that their status in life was secure.

What Sabeer did, as had been done by Jerry Yang and David Filo of Yahoo or Jeff Bezos at Amazon, was to return the cutting edge of ideas to the reasonably intelligent, superachieving everyman. What was Yahoo to start, but a yellow pages? What was Amazon, but a bookstore?

You don't have to be a genius.

You don't have to be superhuman.

You don't even have to be a techie.

Just have an idea.

And the best ideas are right under your nose.

Nowadays, meet Sabeer at a party and ask what he does, and he will tell you only that he works in high tech, just like hundreds of thousands of other young people in the Valley. Sabeer is just twenty-nine years old, and he has a very regal air; he is a deep listener, a gentle giant. He wears chambray shirts over a stocky frame and metal-rimmed eyeglasses. Push him for more detail about his job, and he'll say he works at Hotmail. Ask if he's an engineer and he'll say no, he's the president. He's not being reclusive or coy, it just hasn't sunk in that he might be special.

What is Hotmail but e-mail on the web?

In just under two and a half years, Sabeer has built Hotmail's user base faster than any media company's in history—faster than CNN's, faster than America Online's, faster even than the audience grew for *Seinfeld*. Truly mind-boggling. By the summer of 1998, with 25 million active e-mail accounts, the company was signing up new users at a rate of 125,000 *a day*. Most Internet companies experience a summer slowdown as the country spends more time outdoors and less time online, but in June and July of that summer Hotmail's sign-up rate *increased*.

One night I met Sabeer for a glass of sweet Indian rum at his apartment in Bayside Village, South of Market. Bayside Village is a five-story, three-dimensional crossword puzzle of boxy apartments. His humble apartment has a bachelor pad décor with unadorned white-Spackled walls, a framed print leaned up against the living room wall, a rug rolled up off to the side. His living room has a 180-degree panoramic view of other apartment units, but if you stand in one particular place and stretch your neck, you can get an actual view of the shallow end of the communal pool. It's the same apartment he had the night he wrote the Hotmail business plan. It's definitely not the place I expected from a man who's worth a couple hundred million dollars.

Sabeer believes in the philosophy of Hinduism, which he describes as a belief system different from any other—yet one that, I observed, distinctly parallels entrepreneurial philosophy. "With Hinduism, there is nothing to recite, no rituals to practice. There is no church, no temple. Hinduism is just a way of life. You define for yourself how to live your life. Aided and abetted by your conscience, you define for yourself what are the rules. And if you follow those rules, you

are a Hindu." The rules Sabeer has defined for himself
are to be kind to fellow humans, to respect their indi-
viduality, and to have the discipline to do everything in
moderation.

Still, though, why hasn't he bought a house—even a
moderate one? Is it that he hasn't had time to look? No,
he's looked plenty. "They're just all so overpriced," he
remarks. "I think I'll save a little money if I wait until
they come down."

Beside the couch is a stack of industry trade magazines. At night he sits here, reading these magazines,
trying to digest the chaotic splendor of the Internet.
That's his pipeline of strategic info; he doesn't hire spies
or pay for special insider research. Just magazines, the
same ones you can buy. Available on any newsstand.

The big story of Silicon Valley is continuously being
told and retold, skewed this way and that. It's the story of
rags-to-riches success, and Sabeer Bhatia's story is one of
its prime examples. The variable that differs is whether
the success is due to the individual or the environment—
to personal greatness or circumstance. The story that
gets told most often—ten thousand times a day, this story
gets retold—is the story of Bill Gates. For every time it
is told as the story of an ordinary smart guy who could
never have accomplished very much without the advantage of an operating system monopoly, it is retold as one
of an amazing genius for strategy who has outwitted his
competitors' every end run.

I hear it all the time about Sabeer—with any
Silicon Valley success, there's an analytical community
constantly debating the verdict of history, a chattering
class fuming with jealousy. It's the Valley's restatement
of the nature-versus-nurture question. One side argues,
"Hey, if the big thing he did is just get first-mover advantage on an idea that anyone could have, then he's just a

right-place/right-time lucky Joe." The other side argues, "Hey, any big company could have copied his idea and spent millions on advertising and walloped him, but he made all the right moves to avoid that fate, and that takes great talent. It must be something innate."

So is he great or is he lucky?

Just over ten years ago, on September 23, 1988, Sabeer Bhatia arrived at Los Angeles International Airport at 6:00 in the evening. His flights from Bangalore, India, had taken twenty-two hours, and he was starving. Cal Tech, which had offered him a very rare transfer scholarship, had sent him directions that said merely, "Take a shuttle to campus," but Sabeer didn't know what a "shuttle" was. He was nineteen. In his pocket he had $250, the limit Indian customs allowed a student to take out of the country. He didn't know a single person in all of America. He had won the transfer scholarship to Cal Tech by being the only applicant in the entire world (there are usually about 150 who give it a try) in 1988 to get a passing score on the notorious Cal Tech Transfer Exam, a test full of brain stumpers so challenging that the Cal Tech undergraduate admissions officer told me, "Even most students with a math SAT score of eight hundred will do abysmally." Sabeer had scored a 62. Out of 100. The next highest score was a 42.

Sabeer intended to get his degrees and then to go home to work, probably as an engineer for some very large Indian company. He was following the modest path of life as set by his parents. His mom was an accountant at the Central Bank of India for her entire career, and his father spent ten years as a captain in the Indian Army, then became a manager in several public sector hierarchies. That was what life offered him. India is a very bureaucratic country, so kids like Sabeer grow up presuming that starting a company is impossible unless you are a superhuman.

But as a graduate student at Stanford, when most of his classmates would toss a Frisbee during lunch on nearby Roble Field, Sabeer was drawn to the basement of Terman Auditorium. There were being held brown-bag luncheons, and the speakers were entrepreneurs like Scott McNealy, Steve Wozniak, and Marc Andreessen. Their fundamental message was always the same: *You can do it too.* Sabeer knew that famous people always say such things. They want to be inspirational. But Sabeer's impression of these successful entrepreneurs was that they really were fairly ordinary smart guys, no different from him and his classmates. Sabeer was catching the bug.

When he graduated, Sabeer did not want to go home. So, along with Jack Smith, he took a job at Apple Computer. His parents were pleased—at such a big and important company, Sabeer could work for twenty or thirty years. But Sabeer had started attending cocktail parties of TIE, The IndUS Entrepreneurs, where he met many other older men who had come from India and succeeded here. And again, they seemed like such ordinary guys! Sabeer got swept up in the decade's fever: you haven't lived until you've gone solo. Every morning Sabeer would come in to work at Apple, stop by Jack Smith's cubicle, and tell him yet another story of some guy who'd sold his company for millions. "Jack! What are we doing here, wasting our lives?" But Jack was a shy person and had a wife and two kids to think about. Starting their own business was daunting; they were just two cubicle dwellers buried in the Apple bureaucracy, what did they know about running a business? They were not even managers. Finally, though, Sabeer wore him down: "Jack, given the enormous opportunities here, if we can't make it here, then we are complete failures."

At an IndUS Entrepreneurs dinner, Sabeer sat down one night beside a man named Farouk Arjani. Arjani had been a pioneer in the word processing business in the 1970s, and had since become a special limited partner of Sequoia Ventures. The two hit it off extremely well, and Arjani became Sabeer's mentor. Arjani says, "At first I was amused by him. What really set Sabeer apart from the hundreds of entrepreneurs I've met is the gargantuan size of his dream. Even before he had a product, before he had any money behind him, he had become completely convinced that he was going to build a major company that would be worth hundreds of millions of dollars. He had an unrelenting conviction that he was not just going to build a run-of-the-mill Silicon Valley company. But over time I realized, by golly, he was probably going to pull it off."

In mid-1995, Sabeer began shopping around a two-page executive summary business plan for a net-based personal database called JavaSoft. The venture capitalists were skeptical of the software market, though—too hard to get good distribution and rise above the fray. When Jack and Sabeer came up with the Hotmail idea in December, JavaSoft became, in effect, the front for Hotmail. Sabeer knew that Hotmail was such an explosive concept, he didn't want a less-than-ethical venture capitalist to reject him, then turn around and copy his idea. He kept showing JavaSoft and showed Hotmail only to those VCs he had gained respect for. "It was fine that they were rejecting JavaSoft. But in so doing, I got to see how their mind worked. If they rejected JavaSoft for stupid reasons, then I said thank you and left. If they rejected it for the right reasons, then I showed them Hotmail."

"It's almost embarrassing to admit," says Jack Smith. "We hoped we'd make a little money on the JavaSoft product while we evolved this new thing."

At Sabeer's first presentation to Steve Jurvetson of Draper Fisher Jurvetson, things weren't going well—Jurvetson was having the same problems with the database idea every other VC was. But he was rejecting it for the right reasons. So, late in the hour, Sabeer played the Hotmail card. He mentioned it ever so subtly, characterizing it as a marketing tool. ("Everyone who used Hotmail would wonder how we built it and come buy our JavaSoft tools," he said.) Jurvey wasn't fooled—he saw the pot of gold.

It's fair to say that many investors found Sabeer's headstrong determination as arrogance. Jurvetson remembers, "Sabeer brought in these revenue estimates showing that he was going to grow the company faster than any in history. Sure, most entrepreneurs have that trait, but they also are concerned with looking like the fool. We dismissed Sabeer's projections outright, but he insisted, 'You don't believe we're going to do that?' He had hallucinogenic optimism. He had an unquenchable sense of destiny. But he was right. He grew the subscriber base faster than any company in the history of the world."

One might have presumed that since Sabeer had been rejected by twenty previous VCs and was virtually a nobody, he would be grateful to accept Draper, Fisher, Jurvetson's $300,000 on their terms. "He's the most interesting negotiator I've ever met," Jurvetson says. Tim Draper made the perfectly reasonable offer of retaining 30 percent ownership on a $1 million valuation. Sabeer held out for double that valuation—their cut, 15 percent. Their negotiations got nowhere, so Sabeer shrugged, stood up, and walked out the door. His only other available option was a $100,000 "friends and family" round that Jack Smith had arranged as a backup—not nearly enough money. "If we'd gone that route, Hotmail wouldn't exist today," says Jack. "I still sometimes can't believe he had the guts to walk out of that room."

Draper and Jurvetson relented; they called back the next day to accept their 15 percent.

It took an off-the-charts degree of confidence to do what Sabeer did: first, to hide his real idea, and second, to hold out for the valuation he thought the company deserved. Both are extremely rare. But Sabeer refuses to give the credit to anything other than the culture of the Valley itself: "Only in Silicon Valley could two twenty-seven-year-old guys get three hundred thousand dollars from men they had just met. Two twenty-seven-year-old guys who had no experience with consumer products, who had never started a company, who had never managed anybody, who had no experience even in software—Jack and I were hardware engineers. All we had was the idea. We didn't demo proof-of-concept software or a prototype or even a graphic printed on a piece of paper. I just sketched on Steve Jurvetson's whiteboard. Nowhere in the world could this happen but here."

Sure, but don't famous people always say such things?

This is how the entrepreneur mindset works: Did being turned down by twenty different venture capital firms undermine Sabeer and Jack's confidence? Nope. It just made them burn, it just made them work even harder to prove everyone else wrong. The very impossibility of what they were doing created its own motivation.

In order to keep the idea under wraps, Sabeer and Jack put the JavaSoft name on the front door of their first tiny office in Fremont, California. From February to July 1996, every morning Jack would come to work, log on to the Internet, and search around to see if someone had beat them to it. It always astounded him that he didn't find competition. He was sure Hotmail was too good an idea for them to be the only ones working on it.

The $300,000 was intended for the proof-of-concept version, usually a software system that works on a small scale only and without all the bells and whistles. But Sabeer was so adamant about not giving up more of the company than he had to that he stretched $300,000 farther than it had ever been stretched. Still obsessive about secrecy, they needed a paper-shredding machine, so Sabeer bought the cheapest one he could possibly find, for fifteen dollars. Without any collateral to offer, Sabeer convinced Imperial Bank to loan him $100,000 unsecured. Then he convinced McLean Public Relations to represent Hotmail in exchange for stock, even though he didn't have a product and he was insistent that they couldn't get started on the PR because he had to keep it secret. Montrese Etienne of McLean remembers, "In casual conversation he was always so nice and friendly, and then we sat down to negotiate on the stock, and this riveting fierce aura swept over him, it was almost scary. He became tremendously passionate, almost like another person."

In June, Sabeer was running out of money, but the product would be ready to launch in a month. This is exactly how venture capitalists love to play it—they love to get an entrepreneur into a desperate situation, so they can exact greater ownership for their next round of financing. Sabeer had been in contact with Doug Carlisle at Menlo Ventures, and Carlisle had expressed interest. Sabeer called Farouk Arjani, who told him only to do what he believed. This conversation reenergized Sabeer, though Arjani would later say that he had worried for Sabeer and felt bad for him, and admitted that if he'd been in Sabeer's shoes he never could have cut it so close. "The moment was prophetic of Sabeer's confidence," Arjani said. Sabeer knew that if he launched the service first, he would keep all the leverage over investors. Sabeer convinced all of his first fifteen employees to work only for stock options, not a very common occurrence in a place where the unemployment rate is nil and most jobs come with both pay *and* stock.

"My greatest accomplishment," Sabeer says again and again, "was not to build the company but to convince people that this is their company. I showed people how this would ultimately benefit themselves. My role is as an enabler. No individual made this happen. I didn't do the work. We initiated the avalanche."

They launched on July 4, 1996—Independence Day. It was a fitting date, because Sabeer and Jack believed that free e-mail was a great populist tool. By then, everyone who owned a computer had e-mail, but with web mail you no longer even had to own a computer— you could log on from a McDonald's in Czechoslovakia or a cafe in Taiwan. That morning, Sabeer and Jack wore hip beepers, which they had programmed to flash every hour with the number of new subscribers. The first users found Hotmail all by themselves, but those who found it told their friends: a hundred in the first hour; 200 in the next hour; 250 in the third. The idea was so intuitively powerful that 80 percent of those who sign up for Hotmail say that they learned about it from a friend. It introduced the concept of "viral marketing," in which each e-mail message sent from a Hotmail account was, in effect, an advertisement for the service to its recipient. The service did not need the marketing budget that had originally been anticipated. Sabeer spent a few thousand dollars on some advertisements in college newspapers but then never spent another advertising dollar for the next two years.

By the time Sabeer went back to Doug Carlisle at Menlo Ventures to say in effect *okay, now I need your money*, Hotmail had 100,000 subscribers. His ploy of walking out of the room on Steve Jurvetson had increased the company's valuation by a million dollars, from one million to two. This ploy of stretching the money an extra two months increased the valuation by *$18 million*. So is he really so lucky? "Sabeer may come from a rather ordinary background," says Carlisle, "but he is a very extraordinary individual."

Hotmail began to deliver news and other content right into the e-mail boxes of its subscribers. This was nothing new, but the way the money flowed was. The content sites took the position, "Hey, if you want our news for free, then you'd better pay us." Sabeer refused and wanted it the other way around. He figured that a site's appearing on Hotmail was, in effect, a great teaser advertisement. His users would read the bulletin and go visit that site. He wanted the sites not only to give him free content but to pay Hotmail for the privilege of having it run. Sabeer instructed his director of business development, Scott Weiss, to make sure money flowed into Hotmail, not out of it.

"He would present partnership deals to the board of directors," says Steve Jurvetson, "and we would be amazed. 'How did you possibly get the partner to agree to these terms?' we would ask." The answer was always the same: partners had bought into his vision. He convinced them.

And again, Sabeer was right. Hotmail was growing so fast that some content providers couldn't handle the traffic that came in from Hotmail.

Sabeer was not a micromanager. He gave his people all the opportunities they could handle. "You can tell a lot about an entrepreneur by the quality of people he attracts to work with him," says Doug Carlisle. "If he is attracting strong, smart people, that's a good sign of true leadership quality."

What Sabeer did was get everyone in the company totally focused: telling the same story, harmonizing. That's the essence of what a leader in this business does. It may not sound particularly showstopping, but if you've ever been in a company where the engineers refuse to sign on to delivery dates because they fear they're being set up to fail by the marketing department, which doesn't want to take its share of the blame if the product is late— when harmony breaks down into cacophony, all minds grind to a halt. Nobody's productive. Mental energy is diverted to infighting. Getting everyone harmonized can make all the difference.

Sabeer also spent a great deal of time networking with people. When Sabeer and Jack started approaching VCs, one of their problems was that nobody could vouch for them. There wasn't that "friend of a friend" referral that puts moneybags at ease. If it's true that in the Valley you need Rolodex Power to pull strings and cut deals fast, how do we reconcile that with Sabeer's notion that any twenty-seven-year-old kid with a good idea can make it big here?

The answer is, any kid with a good idea can make it big—as long as he networks like crazy. The only kinds of people the network discriminates against are those who turn their noses up at networking. So it's a meritocracy but a perverted one, based more on the merit of how well you knock on doors than the merit of your Java code. "Every morning Sabeer would come to work," says Jack Smith, "straight from a breakfast meeting. Then lunch with someone else, and after work put on a suit to have dinner with a third person. He likes that kind of thing. He's good at it."

Every morning, Jack Smith still scoured the Internet for signs of competition, and it continually amazed him that there was none. It was six months before the first tiny competition appeared, a one-man company out there in cyberspace. It was almost a full year before Four11's Rocketmail was launched.

In December 1997, Sabeer and Scott Weiss went to Ming's restaurant to watch a presentation by Jerry Yang, the cofounder of Yahoo. Yang talked mostly about what has come to be called, in Internet strategy, "first-mover advantage," referring to the priceless benefits of being the center of attention for a while. Yang said that Yahoo had had a three-month jump out of the gate before he had seen his first competitor, and it was that lead that was responsible for Yahoo being the number one Internet search directory to this day. Sabeer was listening, and his eyes got really big as it dawned on him what that meant.

He'd always been concerned that Hotmail could be copied. He still had only twenty-five employees, a tiny operation. When they were shopping Hotmail to VCs, the objection Sabeer kept getting was, "What's to keep Microsoft from copying the concept and eating you for lunch?" And as they were engineering the system, friends shook their heads and smirked for the same reason: "Like riding a tricycle in the headlights of an eighteen-wheeler." After Sabeer and Jack launched Hotmail on July 4, 1996, industry handicappers predicted, "Another bug about to be squashed on the Microsoft windshield." The gossip rose to a level of outright scorn for Sabeer's foolishness.

Listening to Jerry Yang, Sabeer gained confidence. He leaned over to Scott Weiss and said, "We have a six-month lead in our market. We're going to cream these guys."

"By the time Microsoft figured it out," Sabeer says, "we had six million users."

When Microsoft came bidding in the fall of 1997, it came as a small army. Six at a time, they flew down from Redmond and sat in Hotmail's small conference room across the table from Sabeer. They offered a figure that would have put tens of millions of dollars into Sabeer's pocket. Sabeer rejected it, and they stormed out. A week later they were back, and every week thereafter for two months. At that point, it's easy to see it all as funny money—when you've got a week to think about it, it's hard to really see the difference between $50 million and $60 million. Are you really going to risk losing the deal for another $10 million?

They asked Sabeer to fly up to Redmond. He took Jack Smith and another manager, Steve Dowdy. They were escorted around campus, had lunch with a senior vice president, were shown the building devoted to e-mail and the building devoted to the NT operating system. Their meeting with Bill Gates was scheduled for 2:00 p.m. in a building that is mazelike, notorious for causing visitors to get lost. Sabeer got lost. He arrived just in time. Gates had just gotten back from Russia and was wearing a brown sweater and very-thin-soled Italian shoes. Gates also had with him two senior managers. They all shook hands. There were no ten minutes of get-relaxed time chatting about the flight, the lunch—one of the managers, Laura Jennings, just dropped the ball right on Sabeer. She said, "Sabeer, why don't you tell us about your company?" Sabeer wasn't quite prepared. He began nervously. He couldn't believe it, here he was talking to Bill Gates.

After about fifteen minutes, Gates began to ask questions. Gates is legendary for his Socratic method of picking on the weaknesses of business ideas. "But his questions were very normal strategy questions," Sabeer says, "the same things I had been asked by investors all along, from day one. And it suddenly occurred to me that Bill Gates is not superhuman either. He's human. He's flesh and blood, same as me. He's very smart, yes. But not superhumanly so."

With this understanding, Sabeer became very relaxed. He was completely reoriented, and the meeting lasted until 3:30.

Two stories floated around Hotmail as the talks went on. The first story had run in the *Wall Street Journal*, reporting that in the early days of America Online, Steve Case had spurned an offer from Bill Gates to buy the company. Case had gone on to grow AOL into a company with a multibillion-dollar valuation. This story was photocopied and passed around. It inspired Sabeer. It reminded Jack Smith that Hotmail would be fine even if the deal with Microsoft never came to fruition.

The second story floating around was of what had happened to Pointcast, the push technology innovator, since it had rejected News Corporation's $400 million acquisition offer. Push technology had its fifteen minutes of fame, and then Pointcast fell back into the cacophony. Pointcast was struggling, its plans for an IPO put on hold.

Sabeer took a straw poll among his investors to see what price they might be able to anticipate. Doug Carlisle's figure, $200 million, was the lowest. Privately, Sabeer had half jokingly been saying he wanted a billion dollars, so he challenged Carlisle's figure: "You don't think we can get more than that?" Carlisle laughed, rolled his eyes, and said, "Sabeer, if you ever reach even my figure, then I'm going to build a life-sized bronze sculpture of you and put it in my front lobby."

Sabeer went back to Microsoft with the price of half a billion. "You're crazy!" his adversaries shouted, following it with expletives. "You're out of your mind! You've blown it!" But Sabeer knew those were only tactical outbursts.

As a kid in Bangalore, Sabeer had watched family servants haggling over groceries at the bazaar. He knew every trick. At the bazaar, the vendors would counter a low offer by saying, "Oh, I'm sorry, is that all you can pay? You must be very poor. I feel sorry for you. I want to give you a few rupees out of my own pocket so you have enough money to pay." Tensions were rising as Microsoft piled cash on the table. $200 million. $250 million. Carlisle took to saying, "It's Statue Time!" $300 million. This negotiating squad seemed to have a lot of "deep knowledge" about Rocketmail, Hotmail's competitor, and it was possible that Microsoft was negotiating to buy Rocketmail as an alternative. Or maybe it just wanted to scare Sabeer, to make him think it had another option. Sabeer, who had the go-ahead from his board and management team to negotiate the deal himself, stood firm: no sale. Several times, Microsoft's negotiator pounded the table and stormed out. Although the negotiations were secret, Hotmail's employees twice pressured Sabeer to accept Microsoft's most recent offer and guarantee their security. Sabeer's venture capitalists, who stood to realize gigantic returns on their investments, urged him to be careful.

Negotiating alone allowed Sabeer to present a unified front; it prevented Microsoft from taking Jack Smith to dinner and saying, "Jack, you've got a wife and two kids—c'mon, they'll be set for life." But Sabeer wasn't psychologically alone; his backers and colleagues kept the faith. VC Steve Jurvetson joked with Sabeer, "You don't have to sell now. Why don't you wait until you're big enough to buy Microsoft, rather than them buying you?" All the while, Hotmail kept signing up subscribers. Its lead over its imitators was increasing.

Sabeer would barely budge from his internal sense of what Hotmail was worth. When the negotiation team offered a figure of around $350 million, though, Hotmail's management team took a straw poll in favor of accepting, and then Sabeer was really alone. He cannot give the credit for this one to his talented employees or to Silicon Valley's culture.

"Saying no to that offer was the scariest thing I ever did," Sabeer says. "Everybody had told me, 'This is on your head if you screw it up.'"

On New Year's Eve 1997, a deal was announced. Sabeer is forbidden to state the price, but the S3 registration papers filed a month later stated that ownership of Hotmail had been exchanged for 2,769,148 shares of Microsoft. At the time of the deal, those shares were worth a walloping $400 million. Throughout the Valley, the gut reaction was shock: no way was the company worth so much—$400 million—for *e-mail*? The figure seemed out of proportion, and on its face undeserved, no matter how smart Sabeer may have been, no matter how hard he and Smith had worked, no way was two years' worth of work worth $400 million. There was a sense that Microsoft had gone wacko. Who was this kid, Sabeer Bhatia, and how had he done it?

This "He didn't deserve it" hubbub was particularly loud in the somewhat insular community of Apple and ex-Apple employees, which is where I heard a lot of it. "We weren't doing any great things at Apple," says Jack Smith. "We bummed, we drank, we brought up factories. And that's how people there remember us. With our success we blew away everyone we knew. They still can't believe it. 'What's the deal here? What the hell happened?'"

Farouk Arjani turns that logic on its head: "Sabeer had never had an opportunity to raise money, never had the opportunity to run a company or even a division. But when all was said and done, he did an outstanding job. Certainly, nothing in his background prepared him for it, so it must be something innate in him."

There's no doubt that Sabeer's success has provoked furious jealousy. People here need to believe in a meritocracy, they need to believe success is possible for themselves, and so they will insist that Sabeer is no better than anyone else around town—ordinary, in fact—even though they've never met him and don't know his story. When the Valley gradually learns how Sabeer stood up to his venture capitalists and then stood up to Microsoft, the verdict of history will be kind.

The other unsolicited comment I used to hear all the time is that Hotmail is nothing special, engineering-wise. I believe this comment is similarly superficial. Sure, if you go to Hotmail on the web, it doesn't appear particularly special. The service offers fewer features than the e-mail software that comes free with an Internet account. But in the Internet era, features are not the test. What Jack Smith had to engineer was a system that continued to *scale*, meaning not to crash as it grew in number of users. And it was growing faster than any other media company in history.

Doug Carlisle is holding true to his word about the bronze statue; he has commissioned a bust by an artist in Los Angeles. It's such an odd thing. It seems to me out of character, celebratory of the individual rather than the company or the Internet or the Valley culture. But

Carlisle commonly offers his entrepreneurs such gifts when they reach milestones—a Porsche Carrera, say, or "If you make that, I'm going to kiss your shoes."

If anyone deserves it, I guess Sabeer does. But doesn't it make him uncomfortable? No. "It is an honor. My hope is that, just as I was given inspiration at those brown-bag lunches in Terman Auditorium, when entrepreneurs come into this most prestigious address on Sand Hill Road, it will give them inspiration."

Sabeer has always told his investors that, be it venture capitalists or Microsoft, "If you can find someone better than me to run this company, I will happily step down." As much as Sabeer makes out that he is just ordinary flesh and blood, no one has ever questioned his leadership. He is one of the few valley entrepreneurs to remain his company's top executive beyond the 100-plus employee level rather than being moved off to some nether position as research guru or poster-boy spokesperson.

As of this writing, Hotmail has 144 employees, and it is a subdivision of a Microsoft superdivision called Web Essentials. Hotmail will move from its low-slung, anonymous offices in Sunnyvale to a new Microsoft campus in Mountain View, where it will be joined by WebTV. Sabeer now reports to someone who reports to Bill G., and he flies to Redmond in the middle of most every week.

With Microsoft's financial muscle now behind the company, Hotmail's juggernaut appears unstoppable. In the summer of 1998, Sabeer Bhatia invited me to sit in on his Tuesday-afternoon strategy session with his senior managers. He doesn't interrupt, and he doesn't interrogate or flex his power in the meetings—if he wants to raise a contrary opinion, he will ask benevolently, "Does anyone question that the search box should be on every page?" He let the company unfold for me like a play, each manager playing his part. I learned about a new search engine and an e-commerce plan, instant messaging and a universal website sign-on system, which could potentially be leveraged online much as DOS and Windows are leveraged on the computer desktop. The room was aglow with the anticipatory thrill of riding this bullet train up the exponential revenue curve.

At breakfast one morning I asked Sabeer if he felt at all powerful, considering he runs the world's fastest-growing media company. "That is such an odd, foreign concept to me," he said slowly, trying to think in that old paradigm. "When you say 'power,' that conjures to me control, such as having people do what I want them to do. It is just absurd. It is the nature of this medium that if something is a success, it is wildly successful. If you can come up with something that is of great value for just two people, then it is very likely it will also be of value for ninety million people."

Only eight months after the New Year's Eve announcement, Microsoft's $400 million price tag looked to be a bargain, particularly considering that Hotmail's subscriber base had more than tripled in size since the company was purchased. Everyone's buying into the story now. Nobody thinks the price was unjust anymore. Sabeer's internal sense of what Hotmail was worth was absolutely right.

"We often wonder what would have been," says Jack Smith.

"In retrospect, I'm not sure that a billion dollars wasn't the right figure," says Steve Jurvetson.

Meanwhile, Sabeer Bhatia has a three-year commitment to Microsoft, but there is no doubt he relishes entrepreneurism more than management. His passion for the big risk, the gargantuan mission, is unmistakable.

. . .

On the lucky-or-great question, I believe that you don't get to $400 million without a lot of both, and I have every confidence that if he were not here, Sabeer would be leading people somewhere else. But he believes he's lucky to live in this place and time.

Sabeer knows he never could have accomplished this anywhere other than here—certainly not in India, where corruption and political risk undermine investors' confidence in new ventures. "In America, you have a three-year moratorium on Internet taxes for electronic commerce. In India, e-commerce is actually illegal, because of the 1888 Telegraph Act, which forbids using telecommunications for profit. An 1888 law—can you believe it?"

Of Hotmail's 26 million users today, only 558,000 are from India. That it even has that many users is amazing, since there are only 150,000 Internet connections in the entire country. This in a country with one fifth of the world's population. India's telecommunications monopolies are so corrupt that an Internet connection costs around a thousand dollars to set up, compared to the $19.95 here. Even at that price, more than 2 million people have signed up on the waiting list—they're so hungry to get online—but only a portion of those orders has been serviced. The problem seems intractable.

The last time I saw Sabeer Bhatia, it was 1:50 a.m. on a Monday morning, and he was boarding a Korean Air 747 to start a twenty-four-hour flight halfway around the world—first to Seoul, then on to Bombay. He would meet with business leaders in Delhi and later deliver a speech at Internet World there.

Sabeer had thought hard about what he wanted to say to the country he had left ten years before. He had started to get a vision of how India might be transformed. He had gotten his green card only a few months before he started Hotmail. The level playing field of the Internet has convinced him that in the future, young, ambitious people won't have to leave home.

"India is ready for the Internet revolution. You don't have to get a permit to start a business on the Internet. In India, just to open a little restaurant, you have to get eighteen permits."

Sabeer's vision involves TV, which in India is much more common than phone service. First, install a fiber-optic cable from London to Bombay. Second, use TV cable networks to provide local access points. Third, make available a sub-$50 Net device, somewhat like WebTV's. He estimates the project would take about $200 million to pull off.

It is a gargantuan vision, and it is based on the premise that his own greatness does not exist—Sabeer has convinced himself that he is just a product of the Silicon Valley environment—even though the very fact that he is dreaming such an unordinary-sized dream hasn't triggered the realization that maybe he really is exponentially more visionary than others.

"It's a herculean task," he admitted, "but the prospect of changing the destiny of a country motivates me."

I was witnessing what everyone had said of the early days of Hotmail—Sabeer's unquenchable sense of destiny, his nearly hallucinogenic optimism. As a story, it amused me. It was easy to interpret his enthusiasm as a self-induced late-night fancy that would downgrade from quest to cocktail-party conversation in a few days. It was easy to look at it through the Freudian lens: man returns home for his thirtieth birthday intent on saving other young men from the quandary of having to choose between family and self.

But he was right that India is still a sleeping giant. Sabeer seemed tenacious about it; he'd set up numerous meetings with various officials. After he boarded the plane, it occurred to me that, really, what did I know? Was it not possible that I was watching history at its inception? And I thought, by golly, he might just pull it off.

The next day, I was down in San Bruno interviewing an immigrant entrepreneur from Switzerland who had arrived here on a tourist visa with just a few thousand dollars in his bank account. On the day he had arrived, he hadn't known a single person in America. But he had started a company and was in the process of negotiating for venture capital financing. He'd been rejected by a dozen VC firms already, but he still had the faith. I asked him how he managed not to get dismayed. "I heard a story," he said. "I heard that the founder of Hotmail"—and here he mispronounced Sabeer's name—"was rejected by twenty venture capitalists before he got funded." Then he paused, stirred in his chair, and made a leap of faith masquerading as logic: "So if it can happen to him, it can happen to me, no?" Which was almost, but not quite, the same as *if he did it, I can too.*

EPILOGUE: Caging Sabeer up in the corporate life-style couldn't last. He bought a tenth-story apartment in Pacific Heights, then a Ferrari F1355 Spider, and then in March 1999, he quietly left Microsoft to begin a new venture, Arzoo Inc.

FOR DISCUSSION

1. What parallels does Bronson see between Sabeer's Hindu beliefs and "entrepreneurial philosophy"? (88)

2. Why does Sabeer consider his "greatest accomplishment" not building the company but convincing "people that this is their company"? (96)

3. In Bronson's view, to what extent is Sabeer's success due to greatness, and to what extent is it due to luck?

4. At the time Sabeer sells Hotmail to Microsoft, why do some people see his success as "undeserved"? (103) Why does Bronson believe that "the verdict of history" will be kind to Sabeer? (104)

FOR FURTHER REFLECTION

1. Do you agree with Bronson that entrepreneurs like Sabeer return "the cutting edge of ideas to the reasonably intelligent, superachieving everyman"? (87)

2. Why are some people more able to recognize a powerful idea of the kind that motivates entrepreneurs like Sabeer? What are the characteristics of a powerful idea?

Edwidge Danticat (1969–) was born in Port-au-Prince, Haiti, and separated from her parents, who emigrated when she was four. Danticat and her brother were raised by an aunt and uncle and reunited with their parents in Brooklyn, New York, when the author was twelve. She received a BA from Barnard College and an MFA from Brown University. Danticat writes about the Haitian diaspora, political violence and upheaval in her native land, parent-child relations, and the importance of storytelling. Danticat's many books include the best-selling novel *Breath, Eyes, Memory* (1994), a short story collection, *Krik? Krak!* (1995), and the memoir *Brother, I'm Dying* (2007), a tribute to her father and uncle. She is editor of and a contributor to *Haiti Noir* (2011), an anthology of stories all set in Haiti. Danticat was awarded a prestigious MacArthur Foundation Fellowship in 2009.

Papi

It is a cold Saturday morning, 4:00 a.m. My father gets up to go work. He drives what is called a gypsy cab. He has been getting up early on Saturday mornings for the last fifteen years.

"Are you warm enough?" my mother asks with sleep in her voice. "Be careful. Stay alert."

They part in front of my room, my father leaving for his car and my mother going back into their bedroom where she watches him from the window as he sits in the front seat and waits for his engine to warm up.

My father has eczema. He has dark sores all over his body that won't heal. They used to be dime-sized and dark, now they are quarter-sized and raw because he scratches them.

I once took him to a well-respected dermatologist on Park Avenue. Papi thought he had cancer. The doctor performed a biopsy. It wasn't. I then thought that if he drank enough water or used enough skin lotion, the sores would go away, as if he had an extreme case of dry skin, overly dehydrated from the inside.

For years before, my father had gone to doctors in our neighborhood, the ones who charge fifty dollars a visit whether you have insurance or not. In the Park Avenue office Papi felt out of place. There was a very tall model there and a plump girl with braces and bad acne. Papi read his Bible while we waited. When the doctor called him, he was not sure whether to get up or not. He asked me to go into the examining room with him. The doctor let me stay. I saw her chip off a piece of one of the sores, taking one sample from his leg and another from his stomach. When he had to take off all his clothes, the doctor asked me to leave.

Later, my father would ask the doctor why she took no skin samples from the front of his scalp, where all his hair has been falling out. He doesn't know what to make of that. None of the men in his family have ever lost their hair. My father hates losing his hair, or he hates the way he's losing it—slowly. On the way home from the doctor's office, he wondered how his face would look if he had no hair at all on his head.

"Big," I said.

So my father leaves for work that Saturday and every Saturday at 4:00 a.m. There is a lot of business at 4:00 a.m. on Saturday mornings. People are getting out of nightclubs, going home. "At that hour you can get some real drunks," he says.

Once, working on a Saturday morning, my father cut in front of some young guys in a blue van and they shot three bullets at his car. He had a passenger in the back. "I went so fast, red light after red light, until the passenger was safe."

He never tells us those stories directly unless there is some grave evidence, some obvious mark of what happened. When that's the case, he recounts the events at the Monday night prayer meetings, where people take turns going to one another's houses every week. "Even my family has not heard this" he begins, "I didn't want to worry them. But I need to testify to God's greatness so I won't keep it to myself."

There were also two other incidents that my father couldn't keep secret. Three men he had driven to a far-off area in Brooklyn asked him for all his money when he got there. "When they found that he had only a few dollars in his pocket, they hit his face with a crowbar and ran away. His face was bruised and swollen, but given the circumstances, he made out okay. No bones were broken. He was in the hospital only a few hours, most of the time waiting for a doctor to see him.

Another time a man followed him home in a car. My brother André happened to be sitting on the stoop in front of our house and saw this man walking toward my father with his hands buried in his pocket. My father spotted André and shouted, "Call the police." André wanted to keep an eye on Papi, so he walked up to the man. In a more assured voice than my father's, André threatened to call the police and the man walked away.

"This was the first time I'd ever seen Papi scared," André told me and my other two brothers later that day.

I wondered how many of these kinds of incidents have taken place in my father's life over the fifteen years he's been a cab driver. The Park Avenue specialist says that eczema is like your mental state boiling out on your skin. My father always talks about dying. He's sixty years old.

My father was born in a mountain village in Haiti called Beauséjour, which means "a good stay." Recently the Haitian government asked that archivists no longer demand that parents choose between qualifying their children either as *sitwayins*/citizens or *péyizans*/peasants. I was in the car with my father going somewhere when I happened to read this. I asked him about it. He told me that on his birth certificate, it was said he was a *péyizan*.

I don't know very much about the years between my father's birth and his becoming my "Papi." I have gathered only a few patches of information into a small collage, which I have made into my father's past. Our last name was not Danticat before my father's generation. If we were to trace our family back beyond my grandfather, we'd have to use the true family name, which was Osnac. As was sometimes the custom, in the old Beauséjour, my father's brothers and sisters took their father's middle name, Dantica, as their last name. My father was the first Danticat with a *t*, which was carelessly added on his immigration papers when he applied for a visa to come to the United States.

My father moved from Beauséjour to Port-au-Prince when he was twenty-five years old. He worked as a tailor and then a shoe salesman in a store run by an Italian man in Port-au-Prince. Neither he nor my mother will ever say how they met. I don't think they themselves remember. But they will say that they had a long-distance courtship and that at first Papi's family objected because they had someone else in mind for him to marry. But after he met my mother, every weekend when he wasn't working, he went to a small town in Léogane, a few miles from the city, where he pestered my mother until she married him.

I was born five years after my parents wed. For some reason my mother could not conceive until that time, even though they both very much wanted to have a child. Many uncles and aunts have told me that Papi was overjoyed when I was born: he had wanted a girl. A year later my brother André was born. And then in 1971, when I was two years old, my father moved to Brooklyn.

There, my father lived with his brother-in-law, my uncle Justin, and worked two jobs. One of those jobs was in a car wash during the day, where "even in the cold you had to get wet." The other job was in a sweatshop glass factory that "gave you some idea what hell was like." My father made less than a dollar per hour at each job. He remembers when the price of subway tokens went from thirty-five to fifty cents because the glass factory gave him a penny raise. The car wash job paid for his expenses in the United States. The glass factory job paid for our rent and food in Haiti. In two years, Papi had gathered and saved enough money to pay for my mother's passage to the United States, so he sent for her. But because of immigration restrictions, André and I were not able to come along. We stayed with my uncle Joseph and aunt Denise in Haiti. We were separated from our parents for eight years.

My uncle Joseph and aunt Denise very much believed in "spare the rod, spoil the child." Whenever I misbehaved, they would spank me and spank me good. My brother André was sickly and often bedridden, so he never got spanked as much as I did. I recall getting tired of being spanked one day and shouting, "This misery won't last forever. Wait until my father sends for me." I knew that it was my father who had the power to send for people because he had sent for my mother. My protests against spankings were always answered by a threat from my uncle. "Wait until you go to your Papi; he won't put up with that fresh mouth." Slowly, I grew afraid of my father.

My parents visited us in Haiti in 1976. They brought with them a restless toddler (my brother Kelly) and a sweet adorable baby (my youngest brother Karl). My father, who had a smooth face before, had now grown a beard. I remember the beard prickling my face as he said hello to me and crooned, "Look at my girl, look how big she's become." You leave somebody long enough, they're bound to get big, I thought. I yanked myself away from my father. He felt too much like a stranger and I knew he was not going to stay.

In the two weeks they were in Haiti, when my father called to me, I wouldn't come. When he wanted to play, I ran away. Later, my mother—who I went to and played with—would say, "The way you acted scared your father so much. He knew he had to do all he could to send for you kids. Otherwise, we would lose you."

Because of immigration red tape, it took another five years for my parents to show that they could support us and thus be allowed to have us join them in the United States. In 1981, at the airport in New York, my father was cautious before approaching me. He still remembered my reluctance to go near him when he was in Haiti, and he did not want to be rejected again. He let my mother and my brothers say hello first.

"How was the trip?" my mother asked, as she nudged me toward my father and urged me to kiss him.

At that time I remember thinking, Yes! He's my father all right, because just like me he knows how to hold a grudge.

After we'd just arrived, my father stopped working in the factories and began driving a gypsy cab. He started driving the cab because he wanted to keep an eye on my brothers and me during the day—which wasn't possible when he was working in the factory.

In the mornings, Papi would take us all to school. My brothers Kelly and André were in elementary school. I was in junior high school, and the youngest, Karl, was in prekindergarten.

After he dropped us off, Papi would go to work picking up passengers, and then a few hours later he would collect us all from school.

After school, he would buy us pizzas and Twinkies. He always bought ice cream in unmarked transparent plastic buckets, wholesale, so we immediately knew the flavor by looking at the container. Before leaving the ice cream place, Papi would say, "Look, all American kids love this stuff." He watched television commercials to find out what American kids liked.

Once some boys from school took my brother André out of class and brought him to a candy store in a neighborhood he didn't know. They did this to all the Haitian kids at school who did not speak English. These boys told André they'd kill him if he didn't steal some candy and smuggle it out to them where they were waiting across the street from the store. After he took them the candy, André was deserted by the boys. He called the house crying and found my father there. When Papi brought him home, he said, "I thank God I drive a cab because I'm my own boss and I can be here day and night for you children."

Recently, after years of saving, my father and some friends started a car service business. Papi is the general manager. He still drives the gypsy cab because the business is new and struggling, so he doesn't take a salary. Now he also works on Sunday afternoons when he used to watch Créole comedies and professional wrestling matches. My father does not like to accept money from my brothers and me. "It's very hard to be the guardian of other people's dreams. That can crush your own dreams." When he says this, it's hard to tell if he's talking about his past or about our future.

Now every Saturday my father gets up at 4:00 a.m. so he can pick up some passengers before the business opens at 6:00 a.m. My mother sits in the window watching him from their bedroom. She watches him as he turns on the ignition and combs what's left of his hair. The habitual nature of this morning ritual has rendered my father fearless. I am always frightened for him, since a man was found murdered in his car on our block a year ago. When the detectives came knocking on our front door in the middle of the night, my brother Kelly and I screamed "Papi!" until we remembered that he was asleep upstairs.

André always clips newspaper articles about gypsy cab drivers murdered on the job and gives them to Papi, as a not-so-gentle warning for him to be careful, to be alert at all times. Sometimes André posts these clippings in my father's office at the car service so that the other drivers can see them too. My father often pulls them down and brings them home. He leaves the articles on his desk until one of us removes them.

A few years ago, a friend of my father's was murdered in his gypsy cab, leaving behind a wife and four children. Some nights, when my father is late coming home, my brothers and I sit in the dark and talk, thinking about all the people we know about who have died that way. And always my youngest brother Karl says, "The angel of death has brushed Papi close quite a few times."

So now I always look with my mother as my father waits for his engine to warm up. He wraps his body around himself while blowing in his hands. As Papi sits there alone, I think of all the confidential chats he and I have had in the car, which has served as both taxicab and family car. "Talk to your brothers about how they're spending their money. They take a lot for granted. . . . Don't sit next to that man [an old beau] in church. Everyone will think you're back with him."

Now, with our grudge long settled, my father updates me on his insurance policy. He tells me what numbers to call and where the papers are kept. He tells me who owes him money. "In case I go suddenly, you collect." My mother and I are the only ones who are privy to that information. The boys might accidentally say something in passing and embarrass the borrower.

So now I watch as my father prepares to pull out into the cold morning, this Saturday at 4:00 a.m. The dark is menacing when someone you love is about to head out alone in it. His is the only car moving on the street, and soon it will turn away from our eyes.

My father is one of those people who can walk among others unnoticed. Yet he is to me, my mother, and my brothers a big chunk of life itself. When my father is with me, I can never keep my eyes off him. Something between wonder and worry makes me want to be near him so he can tap playfully on my shoulder, a nervous habit he has.

The filmmaker Jonathan Demme directed a short radio drama that I wrote to be broadcast on a station in Port-au-Prince. It was the story of a father who kills himself because he feels he is not living up to his own dreams or his family's expectations of him. Jonathan wanted my father to be in the radio drama. We knew that Papi would never agree to play the father role, which would require that he speak half the dialogue in the story. So we asked him to play a very small part as a factory foreman.

When the time came to record, I was terrified about having my father listen to the voices of the mother and the child in the story. They literally *loved* the father to death. Without realizing it, they drove him to extremes to please them and finally made him feel unworthy of their admiration. I most feared for my father hearing this line spoken by the actor playing the child: "I would rather die than be like my father whose life meant nothing."

Every time the actor spoke the line I saw my father wince. I knew his mannerisms well enough to read his expression. *Is that what she thinks of me?* I scolded myself, repeating the refrain of one of my closest friends, "Why can't you write happy things?"

On that day I wished I had written something happy, something closer to my father, truer to his own life. It's been said that most writers betray someone at some point in their lives. I felt that I had betrayed my father by not writing about a father who was more of a kindred spirit to him. Since I had the choice, I should have created a fighter, a survivor, a man who would never take the easy way out of life because he wanted to see "his children end up well."

In the studio that day, my father sat in a corner and practiced his few lines as the factory foreman. He even joked with Jonathan about finally getting his chance to be the boss. When his turn came. he recited the lines. He went over them a few times before they had the right timbre.

Later, I wanted to explain. In the car on the way home, I said, "Papi, you know it was a story."

He nodded. "Of course, of course. I understand."

I worried that I had wounded him, that somehow he'd feel that everything he's done in his life has been for nothing. But a few weeks later, I saw him put the tape of the radio play in his car, before heading out in the night. He listened and he laughed while waiting for his engine to warm up.

I remembered Jonathan saying, "You should have seen your old man's face in the studio. He was beaming with pride." I could not see it in the studio, but that day as my father sat in his cab listening, I could see that he was seeing the obvious difference between that father and himself.

When I was a little girl, mad at my father for leaving me, I used to have a recurring dream. I was running in a very dense crowd looking for someone whose face I didn't know but whom I expected to recognize on sight. The people in the crowd had no faces except the one man at the very end, who was my father. Never have I seen my father's face so clearly as when I saw it in that dream. Even in person, he's never been so alive yet so serene, so beautiful.

Now, when I look at him over my mother's head through their bedroom window on Saturday mornings at 4:00 a.m., I always have to remind myself not to compare my real father to that dream. The man in that dream was not there. This father is. And as my father is sitting in his car waiting for his engine to warm up, I always wonder, what is he thinking about? Is he thinking about the past, Beauséjour and Port-au-Prince, of that little girl who loved him so much that she was afraid to go near him for fear he might leave her again? Perhaps my father has now surrendered all that to the present, to the car, the engine, the cold, to the itch of balding, aging, and eczema.

I once asked Papi if he ever had any dreams about my brother André and me when we were still young in Haiti.

"Of course, of course," he said, "but there are too many to tell."

He did not just have the kind of dreams that you have while sleeping, he said. He had waiting dreams; he saw our faces everywhere.

"And now every once in a while I see you in my waking dreams," I told him. "One day I would like to write about that."

"Yeah? If that is true, then will you do something for me?" he asked. "When you write about me give me some hair and decent skin. That will make me happy."

FOR DISCUSSION

1. Why doesn't Danticat's father tell his family about the dangerous things that happen to him while he is driving his cab unless there is "some obvious mark of what happened"? (114)

2. Why does Danticat relate all the dangerous incidents involving her father that she knows about?

3. When Danticat's father says that being the guardian of others' dreams "can crush your own dreams," why does Danticat wonder whether "he's talking about his past or about our future"? (119)

4. While her father is recording his part in her radio drama, why does Danticat feel "that I had betrayed my father by not writing about a father who was more of a kindred spirit to him"? (122)

FOR FURTHER REFLECTION

1. Do you agree with Danticat's father when he says, "It's very hard to be the guardian of other people's dreams"? (119) Is it possible to take on this role without crushing one's own dreams?

2. Do the experiences of Danticat's family suggest that the American dream is or is not attainable to immigrants?

Alain de Botton (1969–) was born in Zurich, Switzerland, and moved to England as a child. He studied philosophy at Cambridge University and worked as a television reviewer and journalist; he published his first novel, *Essays in Love* (1993; titled *On Love* in the United States), when he was just twenty-three. De Botton's works offer a mixture of genres and ideas: part self-help guide, part philosophical treatise, and part literary criticism. His books on love, travel, architecture, happiness, and work are acutely detailed observations on modern life, and they usually address a central theme: How can we live better lives? His work includes *The Romantic Movement: Sex, Shopping, and the Novel* (1994), *How Proust Can Change Your Life* (1997), *The Art of Travel* (2002), and *The Pleasures and Sorrows of Work* (2009), from which this selection is taken. De Botton lives in London, where he founded and runs The School of Life.

Career Counselling

1

However powerful our technology and complex our corporations, the most remarkable feature of the modern working world may in the end be internal, consisting in an aspect of our mentalities: in the widely held belief that our work should make us happy. All societies have had work at their centre; ours is the first to suggest that it could be something much more than a punishment or a penance. Ours is the first to imply that we should seek to work even in the absence of a financial imperative. Our choice of occupation is held to define our identity to the extent that the most insistent question we ask of new acquaintances is not where they come from or who their parents were but what they *do*, the assumption being that the route to a meaningful existence must invariably pass through the gate of remunerative employment.

It was not always this way. In the fourth century BC, Aristotle defined an attitude that was to last more than two millennia when he referred to a structural incompatibility between satisfaction and a paid position. For the Greek philosopher, financial need placed one on a par with slaves and animals. The labour of the hands, as much as of the mercantile sides of the mind, would lead to psychological deformation. Only a private income and a life of leisure could afford citizens adequate opportunity to enjoy the higher pleasures gifted by music and philosophy.

Early Christianity appended to Aristotle's notion the still darker doctrine that the miseries of work were an appropriate and immovable means of expiating the sins of Adam. It was not until the Renaissance that new notes began to be heard. In the biographies of great artists, men like Leonardo and Michelangelo, we hear the first references to the glories of practical activity. While this reevaluation was at first limited to artistic work and even then, only to its most exalted examples, it came in time to encompass almost all occupations. By the middle of the eighteenth century, in a direct challenge to the Aristotelian position, Diderot and d'Alembert published their twenty-seven-volume *Encyclopédie*, filled with articles celebrating the particular genius and joy involved in baking bread, planting asparagus, operating a windmill, forging an anchor, printing a book, and running a silver mine. Accompanying the text were illustrations of the tools employed to complete such tasks: among them pulleys, tongs, and clamps, instruments whose precise purpose readers might not always understand, but which they could nonetheless recognise as furthering the pursuit of skilful and dignified ends. After spending a month in a needle-making workshop in Normandy, the writer Alexandra Deleyre produced perhaps the most influential article in the *Encyclopédie*, in which he respectfully described the fifteen steps required to transform a lump of metal into one of those deft and often overlooked instruments used to sew on buttons.

Purported to be a sober compendium of knowledge, the *Encyclopédie* was in truth a paean to the nobility of labour. Diderot laid bare his motives in an entry on "Art," lambasting those who were inclined to venerate only the "liberal" arts (Aristotle's music and philosophy) whilst ignoring their "mechanical" equivalents (such as clock making and silk weaving): "The liberal arts have sung their own praise long enough; they should now raise their voice in praise of the mechanical arts. The liberal arts must free the mechanical arts from the degradation in which these have so long been held by prejudice."

The bourgeois thinkers of the eighteenth century thus turned Aristotle's formula on its head: satisfactions which the Greek philosopher had identified with leisure were now transposed to the sphere of work, while tasks lacking in any financial reward were drained of all significance and left to the haphazard attentions of decadent dilettantes. It now seemed as impossible that one could be happy and unproductive as it had once seemed unlikely that one could work and be human.

Aspects of this evolution in attitudes towards work had intriguing parallels in ideas about love. In this sphere, too, the eighteenth-century bourgeoisie yoked together what was pleasurable and what was necessary. They argued that there was no inherent conflict between sexual passion and the practical demands of raising children in a family unit, and that there could hence be romance within a marriage—just as there could be enjoyment within a paid job.

Initiating developments of which we are still the heirs, the European bourgeoisie took the momentous steps of co-opting on behalf of both marriage and work the pleasures hitherto pessimistically—or perhaps realistically—confined, by aristocrats, to the subsidiary realms of the love affair and the hobby.

2

It was with this history in mind that I became interested in meeting a career counsellor, a professional dedicated

to finding ways of ensuring that work will be synonymous with fulfillment.

An Internet search produced a company called Career
Counselling International, whose website promised help
for those facing "troubling life decisions and occupa-
tional choices." This authoritative claim led me to expect
large and well-appointed headquarters, but the company
turned out to be run from the back of an unassuming
and cramped Victorian home in a run-down residential
street in South London. It featured a small administrative
office and a consulting room with Paul Klee prints and
views of a clotted carp pond and a washing line. The
only full-time employee, Robert Symons, a fifty-five-
year-old psychotherapist, had started the business twelve
years before, and ran it along with his wife, June, who
helped with the accounts and the marking of aptitude
tests. The couple were admirably fond of some of the less
popular vegetables in the English repertoire, for at most
times of the day—even in the early morning—the place
smelt powerfully of freshly boiled cabbage or swede.
Symons had studied psychology at Bristol University,
where he had come under the influence of the human-
istic school of psychology which emphasised creativity
and self-development. In his spare time, he had written
a book entitled *The Real Me: Career as an Act of Selfhood*,
which he had been trying to publish for several years.

Symons was a tall and bearded man who looked as if
he could wrestle a wolf to the ground, but his physical
might belied the patient manner of a priest. In another
era, one imagined him as the curate of a peaceful
rural parish, keeping bees and a tortoise in the garden,
believing in little, but ministering with exceptional
sincerity to the needs of the sick and the troubled. In
the consulting room, we sat facing each other across
a plate of fig rolls, for which he confessed an almost

addictive fondness. So kindly were his eyes, he seemed like someone who would be open to confessions of the most unusual sort. Not even the most extreme quirk of the mind, appeared liable to surprise him or elicit humiliating judgement. I harboured a confused wish for him to be my father.

Three days a week, Symons saw private clients in his house and, on the remaining two, he visited businesses around the country, advising workers about to be laid off or managers who were having difficulty shouldering their responsibilities. He also offered motivational seminars for the unemployed, psychometric testing for interviews and, from a stand at university careers fairs, sessions with graduates preparing to enter the job market.

We agreed that I should observe his working methods over a number of weeks. I would accompany him on his travels and, via a video monitor in the administrative office (with the necessary permissions in hand), observe his consultations with his clients. All he asked in return was that I should recommend him the name of an effective literary agent.

3

Three days later, I was ensconced in a tight cupboard that served for a study, looking at a black-and-white screen showing the events unfolding in the consulting room next door, where the first client of the day had begun summing up her personal history and professional dissatisfactions with a compelling mixture of formality and honesty. There were papers and files stacked up to the ceiling all around me and, on the floor, a bag of Symons's sports equipment, emitting the strong smell of recently used gym shoes. The client's voice could be heard both through the loudspeaker on the monitor and more directly through the walls. It was one of those crystalline, perfectly enunciated English voices, the sort one might acquire growing up in Walton-upon-Thames and graduating with a First in History from Keble College, Oxford. Through a slit in the door, I could see the client's coat hanging in the hall, a rich blue cashmere garment freckled with water, along with a slim leather briefcase.

Three times the client interrupted her own anecdotes, suddenly pushing back her hair and saying, "I'm so sorry, this must be unbearably boring," to which Symons shot back calmly, as if he had been expecting her to say this all along, "I am here only for you." Twenty minutes into the session, the therapist dropped his voice almost to a whisper and asked, with an avuncular warmth, what had become of the spontaneous and excited child the client must once have been. At which, quite without warning, Carol, thirty-seven years old, a tax lawyer, in charge of a department of forty-five in an office near the Bank of England, began to sob, as Symons watched her with his kindly eyes and, outside, the neighbour's cat took a stroll around the carp pond.

After Carol had left, as Symons threw away a pile of used tissues and rearranged the cushions on the couch, he remarked that the most common and unhelpful illusion plaguing those who came to see him was the idea that they ought somehow, in the normal course of events, to have intuited—long before they had finished their degrees, started families, bought houses, and risen to the top of law firms—what they should properly be doing with their lives. They were tormented by a residual notion of having through some error or stupidity on their part missed out on their true "calling."

This curious and unfortunate term had first come into circulation in a Christian context during the medieval period, in reference to people's abrupt encounter with an imperative to devote themselves to Jesus's teachings. But Symons maintained that a secularised version of this notion had survived even into the modern age, where it was prone to torture us with an expectation that the meaning of our lives might at some point be revealed to us in a ready-made and decisive form, which would in turn render us permanently immune to feelings of confusion, envy, and regret.

Symons preferred a quote from M*otivation and Personality*, by the psychologist Abraham Maslow, which he had pinned up above the toilet: "It isn't normal to know what we want. It is a rare and difficult psychological achievement."

4

When Carol returned the following week, she was dressed in a green skirt and T-shirt and seemed a decade younger. Symons apologised for the smell in the room (his wife was making puréed swede with cheesy crust) and suggested that she submit to a small written exercise. He put in front of her three sheets of blank paper headed "Things That I Like," and gave her ten minutes to make a list of everything which came into her head, from the grand to the seemingly inconsequential, while he went off to get them some lemon-and-ginger tea, having always resisted the Freudian injunction against overfamiliarity between therapist and client.

Carol filled in her sheets, often breaking off to look out of the window. She had the strong, almost masculine beauty one might have associated with the wife of a middle-ranking colonial administrator in Uganda in the 1920s.

Symons knew that it was hopeless to try to guide people towards more fulfilling vocations simply by discussing with them directly what they might like to do. Concerns about money and status would long ago have extinguished most clients' ability to think authentically about their options. He preferred for them to return to first principles and free-associate around clusters of concerns that delighted and excited them, without attempting to settle upon them anything as rigid as the frame of a career.

Symons had a metaphor he favoured: in searching for their aptitudes, his clients were to act like treasure hunters passing over the ground with metal detectors, listening out for what he called beeps of joy. A man might get his first intimation that his real interest lay in poetry not by hearing the command of a holy voice as he paged through a book of verse, but from a beep he experienced at the sight of mist over a quiet valley seen from the top of an edge-of-town carpark. Or a politician, long before she belonged to any party or had any profound understanding of statecraft, might register a telling signal when successfully healing a rift between two members of her family.

As it happened, Carol's beeps turned out to be perplexingly varied. Her reveries about what she liked included visiting old churches, giving presents, making things neat, eating in a fish restaurant set up by a friend in Margate, buying old chairs, and reading blogs about economics on the Internet.

Carol and Symons devoted several sessions to interpreting the list, bringing to the task some of the detachment of a pair of archaeologists assigned to study the rubble of an ancient town. The more they talked about the fish restaurant, the clearer it became that it wasn't the place, in itself, that held any special appeal for Carol; what impressed her was the example of someone who had taken the risk to build a business around a personal interest. Symons took from this exchange the word "passion," which he penned on a whiteboard affixed to the back of the door. As for Carol's love of economics blogs, this was with time revealed to be anchored around an enthusiasm for just one particular example dealing with issues of social entrepreneurship. Symons wrote "altruism and business" on the board.

Counsellor and client now turned their focus to envy. Symons was a particular admirer of this feeling, and lamented the way that its useful role in alerting us to our possibilities was too often censored out of priggish moralism. Without envy, there could be no recognition of one's desires. So Symons gave Carol another ten-minute slot to list everyone she most regularly envied—adding on his way out of the room that he didn't care for niceness and that if there were not at least two names of close colleagues or friends on her piece of paper, he would know that she had been evasively sentimental.

Watching these sessions on closed-circuit television, I came to feel that what was unfolding in the damp room next door was of historical significance. Symons had devoted his life to paying an exceptional degree of attention to the most minor feelings of another person. After millennia in which action had been privileged over reflection, and intelligence primarily restricted to the discussion of arid abstract ideas, an ordinary human's everyday confusions had at last found a forum in which they were being accorded the methodical consideration they deserved. Among all the other, better-established businesses catering to elements far down our hierarchy of needs—businesses offering assistance with gardening and cleaning, accountancy and computers—here, finally, was an enterprise devoted to the interpretation of the critical, yet troublingly indistinct, radio-transmissions of the psyche.

Above Symons's desk was a photograph of Michelangelo's unfinished sculpture entitled *"Atlas" Slave*, from the collection of the Accademia Gallery in Florence. In this block of stone, arrested midway on its journey from raw material to museum piece, an as-yet-headless human figure is seen struggling to emerge from a chunk of marble. The partially completed object appealed to Symons as a metaphor for what he believed that career counselling might do for all of us: in Nietzsche's words, help us to *become* who we *are*.

5

A month into my time with him, Symons asked if I might like to follow him on a working trip to the north of England. Our first stop would be Newcastle, where he had reserved a space at a university's careers fair. Two thousand students were expected to wander through a Victorian hall filled with employers from every sector of the economy and Symons would be offering half-hour consultations, with the option of subsequent discussions over the telephone.

The train from London was packed, so the ticket collector—taking pity on us as we stood in the corridor with large bags holding the components of Symons's booth—let us into the first-class compartment, where we sat in deep velour-covered armchairs and were served a breakfast of sausages and eggs. Far from cheering Symons up, however, the unanticipated luxury seemed to bring out a melancholic side in him which I had not previously seen. As the remains of industrial England passed by outside the window, he brooded over the debased state of modern culture and manners. Then, shifting his focus, he spoke of how few people were willing to invest in his services, and how few of those engaged him for more than a single introductory session or opted for anything other than his test-based methods of counselling, on the basis of their cost and speed. Most Britons were resigned to spending their entire adult lives working at jobs chosen for them by their unthinking sixteen-year-old selves, he concluded, while across the aisle, in apparent confirmation of this analysis, a teenage girl languidly leafed through the celebrity pages of *Bella* magazine.

We reached the careers fair just as the doors were being opened, and hurried to assemble our stand. Students streamed in, often in high spirits, travelling in gangs and regularly erupting with threatening guffaws. Their obvious good health and, in some cases, beauty served to suggest that knowledge and experience might not, in the end, be very valuable commodities to take refuge in.

A few passersby picked up leaflets as they brushed past the stand, but most moved on in a hurry, headed for a defence contractor and a supermarket chain across the way. An unprofitable and wearing day seemed to be confirmed when, in the late afternoon, Symons went through a pile of introductory questionnaires that he had handed out only to discover that one of them had been filled in by Søren Kierkegaard. In the box headed "What I would like to achieve in my career," the nascent comic had written, "To overturn the hegemony of pseudo-Christian values and the hypocrisy of the established Danish Church."

We retreated that evening to a joyless Ibis hotel where the dining room had closed due to a flood and, after a cheese sandwich from a petrol station, turned in early.

Matters began to look up the next day, however, when we went to Middlesbrough to visit a windscreen repair company which was in the process of laying off twenty-five middle managers. The bosses had asked Symons to conduct a seminar entitled "Self-Confidence," during which he would lead the redundant workers through a number of exercises designed to help them to imagine an adequate future for themselves. In the morning session, he projected some slides onto a screen: *I can do anything if I put my mind to it. I can be strong and move mountains. I can set myself goals and achieve them. Nothing I have done so far is an indication of the powers that are within me.* These were supplemented by a booklet Symons handed out, containing extracts from the biographies of famous self-made men and women. On the flyleaf was a quote from Leon Battista Alberti: *A man can do all things if he will.*

None of this was easy to watch, and several times I found myself looking awkwardly out of the window at the cafeteria below. I was particularly troubled to hear one participant repeating, under Symons's direction: *I am the author of my own story.* In the bathroom to which I repaired for mental relief, I cried to analyse my discomfort, and yet, in so doing, began to be suspicious of my own stance. I realised that Symons's talk unsettled me because it reflected a disturbing but ultimately unavoidable truth about achievement in the modern world. In older, more hierarchical societies, an individual's fate had largely been decided by the accidents of birth; the difference between success and failure had not hung on a proficiency with the declaration *I can move mountains.*

However, in the meritocratic, socially mobile modern world, one's status might now well be determined by one's confidence, imagination, and ability to convince others of one's due—a possibility of advancement which shone a less flattering light on philosophies of stoicism and resignation. It seemed that one might squander one's life chances because of a high-handed disdain for books with titles such as *The Will to Succeed*, believing that one was above their shrill slogans of encouragement. One might be doomed not by a lack of talent, but by a species of pessimistic pride.

After lunch, Symons took his managers back into the lecture room and offered them a chance to share their hopes for the future, the idea being that a public revelation of this kind would stand as a promise to themselves which would be the harder to break when their confidence wavered. An employee in her early forties, who had been with the company for twenty years, spoke of her ambition to open a tea shop in the village where she had grown up. So strong was her enthusiasm, and so detailed were her plans (the walls were to be hung with pictures of the young Shirley Temple), that it was almost impossible not to feel stirred. I *can* move mountains, she concluded by saying and returned to her seat, to the applause of all the participants.

I felt my eyes fill. I was reminded that whatever over-cerebral understanding we may sometimes apply to our functioning, we nevertheless retain some humblingly simple needs, among them a prodigious and steady hunger for support and love. It was to the archaic part of our personalities that Symons's motivational exercises appealed, the side which requires neither eloquence nor complex logic and which will forgive ungainly sentences so long as they are imbued with the necessary, redemptive doses of hope.

Towards the end of the day, Symons engaged his audience in a discussion about what he called the voices of despair, internalised attitudes emphasising the chances of failure. Many of the participants traced such voices back to an unhelpful parent or a disapproving teacher, someone who, decades before, had subjected them to criticism or neglect. One after another, grown men and women rose to their feet to recount how, when they were barely the height of a door handle, they had suffered some grievous injury to their self-image: a maths teacher had berated them for their poor algebra skills, or a father had said that it was their sister who was good at art and that they should stick to sport instead.

The evidence suggested that the forming of an individual in its early years was as sensitive and important a task as the correct casting of a skyscraper's foundations and that the slightest impurity introduced at a primary stage could possess a tyrannical power to unbalance a human animal until its dying days. To continue to deny the significance of barely perceptible childhood abuses was to manifest the same robust and foolhardy common sense which had once led our ancestors to scoff at the notion that there might be deadly colonies of micro-organisms thriving in drops of saliva no larger than pinheads.

Seen from this perspective, the weight accorded to ideas of nurture and to the development of self-esteem in theories of modern education no longer seemed like a sign that our societies had gone mad or soft. On the contrary, this emphasis was as finely attuned to the demands of contemporary working life as instruction in stoicism and physical bravery had been to the exigencies of ancient times. It owed its existence less to kindness than to practical necessity. Like the rearing methods of every age, it was intended to ensure that the young would be granted the optimal chances of survival in a hostile environment.

6

A few weeks after we returned from the north, I travelled with Symons to an office in central London, where he had been commissioned by an American bank to put some job applicants through a morning's worth of tests. Symons had hoped that this process could be combined with a more informative round of face-to-face interviews, but the bank turned out not to want to expend the requisite time and resources. The tests would be scored overnight and a decision taken on hiring the following day.

Symons's subjects devoted the bulk of their session to filling out the Morrisby Personality Profile, the most respected and widely used of all aptitude questionnaires. Never far from doubting the wisdom of my own career choice, I joined the candidates in the hope of learning more about my working psyche. I searched for exceptions within lists of words and tried to solve visual puzzles and analogies such as "*Heavy* is to *light* as a) *wide* b) *day* c) *jump* is to d) *brick* e) *narrow* f) *house.*"

Two days later, my test results came back from Symons's office in an exclusively bound folder designed to assert the importance of their conclusions. Held up against the subtlety of the psychological exchanges I had observed between Symons and Carol (who had since handed in her resignation from her law firm and applied for a managerial post with a housing charity), the report felt like it had been written by a computer. "The candidate displays average abilities which would render him well-suited to a range of middle-ranking administrative and commercial posts," the document began, before it singled out a particular talent for marketing and a weakness with numbers. "His future may lie in one of the following fields: medical diagnostics, oil and gas exploration, or the leisure industry."

I recognised my desire to submit to the report's conclusions in the hope of quelling my doubts about my future. At the same time, the report failed to inspire any real degree of confidence and indeed, the more I dwelt on it, the more it seemed to signal some of the limits of career counselling as a whole. I thought again about the smells of cabbage and swede in Symons's office. It struck me as strange and regrettable that in our society something as prospectively life-altering as the determination of a person's vocation had for the most part been abandoned to marginalised therapists practising their trade from garden extensions. What should have been one of the most admired professions on earth was struggling to attain the status open to a travel agent.

But perhaps this neglect was only an appropriate reflection of how little therapists can in the end make sense of human nature. An understandable hunger for answers from potential clients tempts many of them to overpromise, like creative writing teachers who, out of greed or sentimentality, sometimes imply that all of their students could one day produce worthwhile literature, rather than frankly acknowledging the troubling truth, anathema to a democratic society, that the great writer, like the contented worker, remains an erratic and anomalous event, no less immune to the methods of factory farming than a truffle.

The true range of obstacles in the way of unlocking our potential was more accurately acknowledged by the German sociologist Max Weber when, in his essay "Science as a Vocation" (1918), he described Goethe as an example of the sort of creative and healthy personality "who appears only once in a thousand years."

For the rest of history, for most of us, our bright promise will always fall short of being actualised; it will never earn us bountiful sums of money or beget exemplary objects or organisations. It will remain no more than a hope carried over from childhood, or a dream entertained as we drive along the motorway and feel our plans hovering above a wide horizon. Extraordinary resilience, intelligence, and good fortune are needed to redraw the map of our reality, while on either side of the summits of greatness are arrayed the endless foothills populated by the tortured celibates of achievement.

Most of us stand poised at the edge of brilliance, haunted by the knowledge of our proximity, yet still demonstrably on the wrong side of the line, our dealings with reality "undermined by a range of minor yet critical psychological flaws (a little too much optimism, an unprocessed rebelliousness, a fatal impatience or sentimentality). We are like an exquisite high-speed aircraft which for lack of a tiny part is left stranded beside the runway, rendered slower than a tractor or a bicycle.

I left Symons's company newly aware of the unthinking cruelty discreetly coiled within the magnanimous bourgeois assurance that everyone can discover happiness through work and love. It isn't that these two entities are invariably incapable of delivering fulfilment, only that they almost never do so. And when an exception is misrepresented as a rule, our individual misfortunes, instead of seeming to us quasi-inevitable aspects of life, will weigh down on us like particular curses. In denying the natural place reserved for longing and error in the human lot, the bourgeois ideology denies us the possibility of collective consolation for our fractious marriages and our unexploited ambitions, and condemns us instead to solitary feelings of shame and persecution for having stubbornly failed to become who we are.

7

In the end, twelve literary agents read Symons's manuscript. All replied politely and with encouragement. *The Real Me: Career as an Act of Selfhood* remains without a publisher.

FOR DISCUSSION

1. According to Symons, why is it difficult for people to know what work they want to do? Why does he consider the idea of a particular "calling" an "unhelpful illusion"? (132)

2. Why does de Botton find it difficult to watch the seminar on self-confidence that Symons gives to the managers being laid off?

3. Why does de Botton want to believe that the personality test he takes will offer him answers, but feel little confidence in its results?

4. Why does de Botton conclude that there is "unthinking cruelty" in the "magnanimous bourgeois assurance that everyone can discover happiness through work and love"? (143)

FOR FURTHER REFLECTION

1. Do you agree with Abraham Maslow that "it isn't normal to know what we want. It is a rare and difficult psychological achievement"? (133)

2. Is it reasonable to expect most people to find fulfillment in their work?

Meghan Daum (1970–) was born in California but grew up on the East Coast, where she graduated from Vassar College and received an MFA in writing from Columbia University. Daum describes herself as "equal parts reporter, storyteller, and satirist," who, by turning her lens to the issues facing her personally—from being in debt and underpaid in New York City to being obsessed with houses and real estate—speaks with the voice of Generation X. She has been praised for her wit and candor, allowing readers to step into her shoes. Her books include *Let the Trinkets Do the Talking: Essays, Abstractions, and Absurdities* (2001); *My Misspent Youth: Essays* (2001), from which this selection is taken; *The Quality of Life Report* (2003), a novel; and *Life Would Be Perfect if I Lived in That House* (2010). Daum also writes a weekly column for the *Los Angeles Times*.

Publishing and Other
Near-Death Experiences

Why can't book publishing be the way it is in books? Where are those heady nights on Beekman Place, those working days on lower Fifth, those underpaid trust-fund girls with the clacking Smith Coronas and the clicking low-heeled pumps from I. Miller? Where are Bennett Cerf's entrepreneurial seeds, Maxwell Perkins's worshipful authors, Mary McCarthy's well-read bedfellows? Where are the editorial assistants lunching frenetically at the Oyster Bar counter? Where are the pneumatic tubes running directly from Vassar and Smith to Viking and Scribners, sucking young English majors down their chambers and depositing them at chewed, wooden desks with tins of lemon drops in the top drawers and manuscripts towering over the "In" boxes? Alas, lament entry-levelers everywhere, the thirties are gone. So are the forties, fifties, sixties, and seventies for that matter.

There comes a time for every aspiring book publisher when she recognizes that her career, though inspired by Mary McCarthy's, will not resemble it. After a few weeks steeped in proposals for self-help books or un-authorized biographies of cable-access television stars, she realizes that there is no longer a May Day parade, the *Nation* is not a publication immediately accessible to twenty-two-year-old English majors seeking reviewer positions, two-bedroom apartments on Jane Street are out of the single girl's price range, and Webster Hall is no longer filled with the literati but with drag queens.

There comes a point when she notices that although she studied Homer, Austen, and Melville, she will not be publishing them. There are a few holdouts from the "literary" camp, to be sure (the assistant may find herself remarking on the fact that here, in the world of books, "literature" is considered a category as specific as "how to" or "occult") but there seems to be a disproportionate number of Oprah bios, guides to better sexual relationships, and Near-Death Experience books, slugged for those on the inside as N.D.E. "A new N.D.E. title," screams the publisher, dollar signs glowing in her contact lenses. "Isn't this to die for?" To the publisher, N.D.E. means big excitement and big bucks. To the assistant it can also stand for "not doing editing," or "not drinking enough."

I've had a number of different editorial assistant jobs. Some of these were on high floors of midtown office buildings, stale and plasticky smelling, the kinds of places where employees fight to assert their identities by tacking Polaroids of boyfriends and cats on their cubical walls. Others were sweet and arty, housed in the sort of loft-like office where the Mia Farrow character in a Woody Allen film always seems to work. Still another office was so mouse infested that I found myself not just tapping but actually stomping my feet underneath my desk for hours at a stretch; it seemed the moment I stopped, a rodent would make its way from the floor to an open desk drawer, wherein I would later fish around for a pen and instead discover something that made me actually weep in disgust and then yearn for a career in investment banking.

For the editorial assistant, every day is a new near-death experience. As if "going toward the light," we chase after what literature there is, trying, at least in the beginning, to discover the genius in the slush pile who's going to elevate us from entry-level minion to the up-and-comer with the brilliant eye. Our job entails pretty much what it sounds like: assisting editors. We open our editors' mail and log in the submissions. We keep track of flap copy and back-cover blurbs. We notice when a typo appears on a jacket mock-up—there's a fine line between *Prozac Nation* and *Prosaic Notion*. We request contracts, fill out invoices, and, mostly, answer the phone again and again. "Candy Whatzit's office," we say. "Jillian Dazzlewitz's line," and then, when our personal line rings with the promise of a friend on the other end or even an author whose manuscript is sufficiently unhot that *we might actually acquire it ourselves*, we answer obediently, with the name of the company, blurted unintelligibly because four other lines are on hold. As all editorial assistants know, it is not acceptable to pick up the phone and deliver a simple "hello." This is a trapping of the editorially privileged, of those with more than one linen blazer and their own offices with radiators upon which cardboard-mounted book jackets are gleamingly displayed. I spent quite a lot of time in my editorial-assistant days dreaming about when I'd be able to answer with a "hello." I even experimented with it intermittently, pulling it out like a pair of torn jeans on casual Fridays. "Hello," I'd say, with faux nonchalance at 7:30 in the evening after everyone had left. This usually resulted in the person hanging up, or my mother's voice emerging on the other end, insisting that such lack of professionalism surely wasn't going to result in a promotion any time soon.

So it's all in the phone greeting, the banter with authors and agents, the art of raising the pitch of our voices when we call the accounting department to ask what happened to that check for the $100,000 advance because the "author is desperately poor and the agent is ballistic." (The truth is that we discovered the check request under a pile of magazines on our desk two months after we were supposed to process it.) But the voice will fix everything. It rises when we're covering up our clerical errors, drops to sultry depths when we're schmoozing or gossiping or ordering a decaf cap (with skim milk) from the deli around the corner. We're secretaries fully versed in Derrida, receptionists who have read Proust in French. This is a land of girls. There are always at least ten of "us" for every one of "him." We've got decent shoes. We've got BAs in English from fancy schools, expensive haircuts, expensive bags, and cheap everything else. We've got the studio apartment with the half-eaten one-hundred-calorie yogurt in the mini-fridge. We've got one message flashing on the answering machine (it's Mom again), bad TV reception, and a pile of manuscripts to read before bedtime. We've got an annual take-home of $18,000 before taxes if we're lucky, a $100 deductible on the health insurance, which is useful about one year into the job when we reach that milestone of entering therapy (inspired by the books we're working on), when we have to remind ourselves that getting out of bed every morning is mandatory rather than optional, when we realize that the phrase "there's a lot of writing involved" as it pertains to a job is subject to interpretation.

Like all legends, the glamour of publishing that we read about in McCarthy's *Intellectual Memoirs* or Mary Cantwell's *Manhattan, When I Was Young* is likely to be shattered somewhere around the first anniversary of assistantship. Though our heroines were no doubt just as burdened by this age-old indentured servitude as we are, there's something in the retelling, in the breezy we-can-laugh-about-it-now quality of such memoirs that today's editorial slaves find confusing. It's as if a sepia tint has been imposed onto a thoroughly fluorescent-lit world. Unlike our predecessors, we find ourselves spending considerably more lunch hours waiting in line at Ess-A-Bagel than sitting at the counter at the Oyster Bar. We realize that we're spending a significant amount of office time changing the fax paper, chasing down botched contracts, and writing flap copy for *Thin Thighs in Three Seconds* rather than inhabiting a publishing world like the one Dan Wakefield evoked in his memoir *New York in the Fifties*, where "the booze ran freely and the talk was always funny, sharp, knowing, dealing with what we cared about most—books, magazines, stories, the words and the people who wrote them."

To the dewy eye of the editorial assistant, there is something about this mythos—the stiff patent leathers tromping around Madison Square, the particular literary drunkenness that seemed obtainable only from the taps of the White Horse Tavern, where Dylan Thomas met the shot glass that killed him—that feels lost, abandoned in nostalgia's inevitable recycling bin. Instead, there are lunches eaten while hunched over a plastic container of tricolored pasta salad from the Korean deli. There are hundreds of hours spent at the copy machine duplicating manuscripts, thousands of phone messages scrawled on carbon message pads, and a few attempts to raise our salaries to something resembling at least the annual tuition fee of the college we attended (not including the cost of books). Nonetheless we persevere, dreaming of the day when we'll become an assistant editor, and wondering how we'll survive the ensuing years until that fabled associate editor position is dangled before our eyes. If we make it this far without ditching the whole thing and going back to school for yet another graduate degree, we, too, could be the star editor responsible for the true story of Howard Stern's near-death experience.

A savory thought, yet one that, like the devil, threatens to drag us down by the sharp lapels of our Burberry raincoats. Its a good thing we don't own any. We can't afford them. Besides, they're not as timeless as they once were.

FOR DISCUSSION

1. Why does Daum refer to "the assistant" or "the editorial assistant" when relating her own experiences in publishing?

2. Why does Daum say that "every day is a new near-death experience" for editorial assistants? (148)

3. According to Daum, why do editorial assistants stay on the job despite its disappointments?

4. Why does Daum describe the idea of becoming a star editor as a "savory thought" that "like the devil, threatens to drag us down"? (152)

FOR FURTHER REFLECTION

1. What is Daum's attitude toward her expectations of the publishing world based on books by Mary McCarthy and Mary Cantwell? Does Daum fault herself for expecting publishing to be as these writers describe it, or does she blame the publishing world for not meeting her expectations?

2. How does Daum feel about being in "a land of girls" where there "are always at least ten of 'us' for every one of 'him'"? (150)

Kiran Desai (1971–) was born in New Delhi, India, and educated in India, England, and the United States. Desai's first novel, *Hullabaloo in the Guava Orchard* (1998), was published while she was still a graduate student at Columbia University; it won the British Society of Authors' Betty Trask Prize for best first novel by an author under thirty-five. Desai's second novel, *The Inheritance of Loss* (2006), won the Man Booker Prize and the National Book Critics Circle award for fiction. Through her use of vivid and distinctive characterization and lush physical description, Desai explores themes of globalization, multiculturalism, economic inequality, postcolonialism, religious fundamentalism, and terrorist violence—revealing how the past continues to shape the present.

The Inheritance of Loss
(selection)

Brigitte's, in New York's financial district, was a restaurant all of mirrors so the diners might observe exactly how enviable they were as they ate. It was named for the owners' dog, the tallest, flattest creature you ever saw; like paper, you could see her properly only from the side.

In the morning, as Biju and the rest of the staff began bustling about, the owners, Odessa and Baz, drank Tailors of Harrowgate darjeeling at a corner table. Colonial India, free India—the tea was the same, but the romance was gone, and it was best sold on the word of the past. They drank tea and diligently they read the *New York Times* together, including the international news. It was overwhelming.

Former slaves and natives. Eskimos and Hiroshima people, Amazonian Indians and Chiapas Indians and Chilean Indians and American Indians and Indian Indians. Australian aborigines, Guatemalans and Colombians and Brazilians and Argentineans, Nigerians, Burmese, Angolans, Peruvians, Ecuadorians, Bolivians, Afghans, Cambodians, Rwandans, Filipinos, Indonesians, Liberians, Borneoans, Papua New Guineans, South Africans, Iraqis, Iranians, Turks, Armenians, Palestinians, French Guyanese, Dutch Guyanese, Surinamese, Sierra Leonese, Malagasys, Senegalese, Maldivians, Sri Lankans, Malaysians, Kenyans, Panamanians, Mexicans, Haitians, Dominicans, Costa Ricans, Congoans, Mauritanians, Marshall Islanders, Tahitians, Gabonese, Beninese,

Malians, Jamaicans, Botswanans, Burundians, Sudanese, Eritreans, Uruguayans, Nicaraguans, Ugandans, Ivory Coastians, Zambians, Guinea-Bissauans, Cameroonians, Laotians, Zaireans coming at you screaming colonialism, screaming slavery, screaming mining companies screaming banana companies oil companies screaming CIA spy among the missionaries screaming it was Kissinger who killed their father and why don't you forgive third-world debt; Lumumba, they shouted, and Allende; on the other side, Pinochet, they said, Mobutu; contaminated milk from Nestlé, they said; Agent Orange; dirty dealings by Xerox. World Bank, UN, IMF, everything run by white people. Every day in the papers another thing!

Nestlé and Xerox were fine upstanding companies, the backbone of the economy, and Kissinger was at least a patriot. The United States was a young country built on the finest principles, and how could it possibly owe so many bills?

Enough was enough.

Business was business. Your bread might as well be left unbuttered were the butter to be spread so thin. The fittest one wins and gets the butter.

"Rule of nature," said Odessa to Baz. "Imagine if we were sitting around saying, 'So-and-so-score years ago, Neanderthals came out of the woods, attacked my family with a big dinosaur bone, and now you give back.' Two of the very first iron pots, my friend, and one toothsome toothy daughter from the first days of agriculture, when humans had larger molars, and four samples of an early version of the potato claimed, incidentally, by both Chile and Peru."

She was very witty, Odessa. Baz was proud of her cosmopolitan style, loved the sight of her in her little wire-rimmed glasses. Once he had been shocked to overhear some of their friends say she was black-hearted, but he had put it out of his mind.

"These white people!" said Achootan, a fellow dish-washer, to Biju in the kitchen. "Shit! But at least this country is better than England," he said. "At least they have some hypocrisy here. They believe they are good people and you get some relief. There they shout at you openly on the street, 'Go back to where you came from.'" He had spent eight years in Canterbury, and he had responded by shouting a line Biju was to hear many times over, for he repeated it several times a week: "Your father came to *my* country and took *my* bread and now I have come to *your* country to get *my* bread back."

Achootan didn't want a green card in the same way as Saeed did. He wanted it in the way of revenge.

"Why do you want it if you hate it here?" Odessa had said angrily to Achootan when he asked for sponsorship.

Well, he wanted it. Everyone wanted it whether you liked it or you hated it. The more you hated it sometimes, the more you wanted it. This they didn't understand.

The restaurant served only one menu: steak, salad, fries. It assumed a certain pride in simplicity among the wealthy classes.

Holy cow. Unholy cow. Biju knew the reasoning he should keep by his side. At lunch and dinner the space filled with young uniformed businesspeople in their twenties and thirties.

"How would you like that, ma'am?"

"Rare."

"And you, sir?"

"Still mooin'."

Only the fools said, "Well done, please." Odessa could barely conceal her scorn. "Sure about that? Well, all right, but it's going to be tough."

She sat at the corner table where she had her morning tea and aroused the men by tearing into her steak.

"You know, Biju" she said, laughing, "isn't it ironic, nobody eats beef in India and just look at it—it's the shape of a big T-bone."

But here there were Indians eating beef. Indian bankers. Chomp chomp. He fixed them with a concentrated look of meaning as he cleared the plates. They saw it. They knew. He knew. They knew he knew. They pretended they didn't know he knew. They looked away. He took on a sneering look. But they could afford not to notice.

"I'll have the steak," they said with practiced nonchalance, with an ease like a signature that's a thoughtless scribble that you *know* has been practiced page after page.

Holy cow unholy cow.

Job no job.

One should not give up one's religion, the principles of one's parents and their parents before them. No, no matter what.

You had to live according to something. You had to find your dignity. The meat charred on the grill, the blood beaded on the surface, and then the blood also began to bubble and boil.

Those who could see a difference between a holy cow and an unholy cow would win.

Those who couldn't see it would lose.

So Biju was learning to sear steaks.

Blood, meat, salt, and the cannon directed at the plates: "Would you like freshly ground pepper on that, sir?"

"You know we may be poor in India, but there only a dog would eat meat cooked like this," said Achootan.

"We need to get aggressive about Asia," the businessmen said to each other. "It's opening up, new frontier, millions of potential consumers, big buying power in the middle classes, China, India, potential for cigarettes, diapers, Kentucky Fried, life insurance, water management, cell phones—big family people, always on the phone, all those men calling their mothers, all those mothers calling all their many, many children; this country is done, Europe done, Latin America done, Africa is a basket case except for oil; Asia is the next frontier. Is there oil anywhere there? They don't have oil, do they? They must. . . ."

The talk was basic. If anyone dared to call them *Fool!* they could just point at their bank accounts and let the numbers refute the accusation.

Biju thought of Saeed Saeed who still refused to eat a pig, "They dirty, man, they messy. *First* I am Muslim, then I am Zanzibari, *then* I *will BE* American." Once he'd shown Biju his new purchase of a model of a mosque with a quartz clock set into the bottom that was programmed, at the five correct hours, to start agitating: *"Allah hu Akbar, la ilhaha illullah, wal lah hu akbar. . . ."* Through the crackle of the tape from the top of the minaret came ancient sand-weathered words, that keening cry from the desert offering sustenance to create a man's strength, his faith in an empty-bellied morning and all through the day, that he might not fall through the filthy differences between nations. The lights came on encouragingly, flashing in the mosque in disco green and white.

. . .

"Why do you want to leave?" Odessa was shocked. A chance like they had given him! He surely didn't know how lucky he was.

"He'll never make it in America with that kind of attitude," said Baz hopefully.

Biju left as a new person, a man full to the brim with a wish to live within a narrow purity.

"Do you cook with beef?" he asked a prospective employer.

"We have a Philly steak sandwich."

"Sorry. I can't work here."

"They worship the cow," he heard the owner of the establishment tell someone in the kitchen, and he felt tribal and astonishing.

Smoky Joe's.

"Beef?"

"Honey," said the lady, "Ah don't mean to ahffend you, but Ah'm a steak eater and Ah AAHM beef."

Marilyn. Blown-up photographs of Marilyn Monroe on the wall, Indian owner at the desk!

The owner was on the speakerphone.

"Rajnibhai, *Kem chho?*"

"What?"

"Rajnibhai?"

"Who aez thees?" Very Indian-trying-to-be-American accent.

"Kem chho? Saaru chho? Teme samjo chho?"

"WHAAT?"

"Don't speak Gujerati, sir?"

"No."

"You are Gujerati, no?"

"No."

"But your name is Gujerati??"

"Who are you??!!"

"You are *not* Gujerati?"

"Who are you??!!"

"AT&T, sir, offering special rates to India."

"Don't know anyone in India."

"Don't know anyone???? You must have some relative?"

"Yeah," American accent growing more pronounced, "but I don' taaalk to my relateev. . . ."

Shocked silence.

"Don't talk to your relative?"

Then, "We are offering forty-seven cents per minute."

"Vhaat deeference does that make? I haeve aalready taaald you," he spoke s l o w as if to an idiot, "no taleephone caalls to Eeendya."

"But you are from Gujerat?" Anxious voice.

"Veea Kampala, Uganda, Teepton, England, and Roanoke state of Vaergeenia! One time I went to Eeendya and, laet me tell you, you canaat pay me to go to that caantreey agaen!"

Slipping out and back on the street. It was horrible what happened to Indians abroad and nobody knew but other Indians abroad. It was a dirty little rodent secret. But, no, Biju wasn't done. His country called him again. He smelled his fate. Drawn, despite himself, by his nose, around a corner, he saw the first letter of the sign, *G*, then an *AN*. His soul anticipated the rest: *DHI*. As he approached the Gandhi Café, the air gradually grew solid. It was always unbudgeable here, with the smell of a thousand and one meals accumulated, no matter the winter storms that howled around the corner, the rain, the melting heat. Though the restaurant was dark, when Biju tested the door, it swung open.

There in the dim space, at the back, amid lentils splattered about and spreading grease transparencies on the cloths of abandoned tables yet uncleared, sat Harish-Harry, who, with his brothers Gaurish-Gary and Dhansukh-Danny, ran a triplet of Gandhi Cafés in New York, New Jersey, and Connecticut. He didn't look up as Biju entered. He had his pen hovering over a request for a donation sent by a cow shelter outside Edison, New Jersey.

If you gave a hundred dollars, in addition to such bonus miles as would be totted up to your balance sheet for lives to come, "We will send you a free gift; please check the box to indicate your preference":

> 1. A preframed decorative painting of Krishna-Lila: "She longs for her lord and laments."

> 2. A copy of the *Bhagavad Gita* accompanied by commentary by Pandit so-and-so (BA, MPhil, PhD, President of the Hindu Heritage Center), who has just completed a lecture tour in sixty-six countries.

> 3. A CD of devotional music beloved by Mahatma Gandhi.

> 4. A gift-coupon to the Indiagiftmart: "Surprise the special lady in your life with our special *choli* in the colors of onion and tender pink, coupled with a butter *lehnga*. For the woman who makes your house a home, a set of twenty-five spice

jars with vacuum lids. Stock up on Haldiram's Premium Nagpur Chana Nuts that you must have been missing. . . ."

His pen hovered. Pounced.

To Biju he said: "Beef? Are you crazy? We are an all-Hindu establishment. No Pakistanis, no Bangladeshis, those people don't know how to cook, have you been to those restaurants on Sixth Street? *Bilkul bekaar. . . .*"

One week later, Biju was in the kitchen and Gandhi's favorite tunes were being sung over the sound system.

FOR DISCUSSION

1. Why does Achootan want a green card even though he hates living in the United States? What does it mean that he wants it "in the way of revenge"? (157)

2. While working at Brigitte's restaurant, why does Biju think, "Those who could see a difference between a holy cow and an unholy cow would win. Those who couldn't see it would lose"? (158)

3. When Biju is looking for a new job, why does he think, "It was horrible what happened to Indians abroad and nobody knew but other Indians abroad"? (161)

4. Why does Biju go to work at the Gandhi Café? Does the story suggest that working there will allow Biju to retain his Indian identity?

FOR FURTHER REFLECTION

1. How does Desai use adherence to or neglect of dietary traditions to comment on the characters' assimilation to new surroundings? Why are these traditions often so important to immigrants?

2. Is it better for immigrant groups to be assimilated into the dominant culture or to retain their traditional cultures? Why are some immigrants willing to give up or change practices when they live in other countries?

Comparison Questions

1. How do Meghan Daum, David Sedaris, and Barbara Ehrenreich use their personal experiences to make a statement about what is going on in the world? What are the strengths and weaknesses of using personal experiences to generalize about larger issues?

2. Do the work experiences of Edwidge Danticat's father support or contradict Alain de Botton's contention that work has become "synonymous with fulfilment"? (130)

3. Compare Bridget's feeling, in "Betting on Men," that she must "pander and lie to men she pitied and deplored—for a barely sufficient wage" with Meghan Daum's and Barbara Ehrenreich's feelings about their work experiences. (58) How much of the experience of these authors is unique to women workers?

4. How does the concept of work in Philip Levine's "What Work Is" compare with work as depicted by Tillie Olsen and Kiran Desai in their stories?

5. What do the experiences of Sabeer Bhatia, in "The Entrepreneur," and Edwidge Danticat's father, in "Papi," say about the factors needed for immigrants to achieve financial success in the United States?

6. What might Barbara Ehrenreich say about the challenges faced by Tillie Olson's narrator in trying to make a living and raise her daughter?

About Shared Inquiry

Shared Inquiry™ is the effort to achieve a more thorough understanding of a text by discussing questions, responses, and insights
with fellow readers. Careful listening is essential. The leader guides
the discussion by asking questions about specific ideas, problems
of meaning, and passages in the text, but does not seek to impose
a personal interpretation on the group.

During discussion, participants consider a number of different
ideas and weigh the evidence for each. Introducing ideas and then
refining or abandoning them are valuable parts of the interpretive
process. Participants gain experience in communicating complex
ideas and in supporting, testing, and expanding their thoughts.
Everyone in the group contributes to the discussion. While participants may disagree with one another, they treat one another's
ideas respectfully.

This process helps participants develop an understanding of
important texts and ideas, rather than merely catalog knowledge
about them. The following guidelines keep conversation focused
on the text and assure that all participants have a voice:

1. **Read the selection carefully before participating in
   the discussion.** This ensures that all participants are equally
   prepared to talk about the text.

2. **Support your ideas with evidence from the text.** This
   keeps the discussion focused on understanding the selection
   and enables the group to weigh textual support for different
   interpretations.

3. **Discuss the ideas, themes, and formal elements in the selection and try to understand them fully before exploring issues that go beyond the selection itself.** Adequate reflection on the selection and various interpretations of it will make the exploration of broader issues more productive.

4. **Listen to other participants and respond to them directly.** Shared Inquiry is about the give-and-take of ideas, the willingness to listen to others and talk with them respectfully. Directing your comments and questions to other participants in the discussion, not always to the leader, will make the discussion livelier and more dynamic.

5. **Expect the leader to only ask questions.** Effective leaders help participants develop their own ideas, with everyone gaining a new understanding in the process. When participants hang back and wait for the leader to suggest answers, the discussion tends to falter.

Acknowledgments

All possible care has been taken to trace ownership and secure permission for each selection in this anthology. The Great Books Foundation wishes to thank the following authors, publishers, and representatives for permission to reprint copyrighted material:

I Stand Here Ironing, from TELL ME A RIDDLE, by Tillie Olsen. Copyright © 1961 by Tillie Olsen. Reprinted by permission of the Frances Goldin Literary Agency.

What Work Is, from WHAT WORK IS, by Philip Levine. Copyright © 1991 by Philip Levine. Reprinted by permission of Alfred A. Knopf, a division of Random House, Inc.

Nickel and Dimed, from "Nickel-and-Dimed: On (Not) Getting By in America," by Barbara Ehrenreich. Copyright © 1999 by Barbara Ehrenreich. Essay first appeared in *Harper's Magazine*, January, 1999. Reprinted by permission of International Creative Management, Inc.

Betting On Men, from IN ENVY COUNTRY, by Joan Frank. Copyright © 2010 by Joan Frank. Reprinted by permission of the author.

SantaLand Diaries, from HOLIDAYS ON ICE, by David Sedaris. Copyright © 1997 by David Sedaris. Reprinted by permission of Little, Brown and Company.

The Entrepeneur, from THE NUDIST ON THE LATE SHIFT, by Po Bronson. Copyright © 1999 by Po Bronson. Reprinted by permission of Random House, Inc.